Tomorrow There is Love

Tomorrow There is Love

Love Secrets for Intimate Relationships

Nick Polimeni

One Spirit Press
Portland, Oregon

© Copyrighted 2011 by Nick Polimeni

All Rights Reserved
Printed in USA

ISBN 978-1-893075-13-9
LCCN 2011921624

Cover Design by Ethan Firpo
Interior Design Spirit Press, LLC

This book may not be reproduced in
whole or in part, by electronic or any
other means which exist or
may yet be developed, without
permission of:

One Spirit Press
Portland, Oregon

Dedication

A legacy to my Stephanie, my future!
A gift to Natalie, whose inquiries set me on this quest!
To Nancy, who knows how to love unconditionally and who embraced the un-embraceable!

With loving recognition to Ali and Cotton for their reviews, interviews, and encouragement, to Tulipldy and Christian, for important feedback on critical sections, and to Firelight for serious scrutiny!

And a heartfelt thank you to the many women who confided, advised, and encouraged me, a few of which are listed, without whose revelations, openness, and willingness to participate in this project, it would never have materialized:

Alhana, Alia, Alikata, Ananda, Axantis, Cher_kee, Christian, Codesa, Cotton, Craven, Crea, DreamOfJeanie, Fire_Light, Gazania, Gent3Soul, Julia, Kalena, LindaF, Lisa, MistaCat, Savannah, Sharandria, Silky, Silkyone, Sol, sugah_tyme, Tulipldy.

Contents

Introduction...vii

Part I–The Fairy Tale ...3

Chapter One–Once Upon A Time...5

Chapter Two–Fast Forward....13

Chapter Three–New Ways To Love.....23

Chapter Four–Meeting People.....37

Chapter Five–Love At First Sight.....45

Part II–Posturing and Positioning 51

Chapter Six–Beauty and The Beast...53

Chapter Seven–Exploring Emotions....61

Chapter Eight–Dating Protocols....73

Chapter Nine–Reading His Heart....89

Part III–The Dawning 103

Chapter Ten–Communication....105

Chapter Eleven–What is Love....115

Chapter Twelve–Charting A Course....129

Part IV–The Shoals and Narrows 141

Chapter Thirteen–Inner Conflict.....143

Chapter Fourteen–Helen, the Face that Launched a Thousand Ships....155

Chapter Fifteen–Violence and Abuse....167

Part V–The Nurturing 179

PhaseChapter Sixteen–The Magic Key....181

Chapter Seventeen–Woman-Mother....189

Chapter Eighteen–The Social Side of a Connection....197

Part VI–The Wisdom 211

Chapter Nineteen–The Break....213

Chapter Twenty–The Road Back....223

Chapter Twenty One–Salvage Operation....231

Prologue - All Good Things...253

Colophon....256

Introduction

I am a man. Who would better know a woman's heart than a sensitive man, one whose heart has been taken over many times by a woman's passion?

The intensity of that passion holds a vibrancy in my mind that prompts me to share the wisdom they've given me, and give it back to them to show each one how to build herself to manifest the power that is sleeping in her inner sanctum; to show her how to heal the wounds that might have closed her heart, and to show her how to resurrect the phoenix within so she can cross the threshold of desire into the world of fulfillment.

In this quiet adventure I propose you undertake, you can and will build the dwelling for your homecoming. You will select each precious component of your life and each little tool necessary to reconstruct that which you know is alive deep inside you, that others have had you look for outside you: happiness, accomplishment, love, strength, and fulfillment. Yes! These things are inside you already and you can bring them back to life.

The wisdom and advice presented here will work for those who, with meticulous care, are earnestly ready and willing to take simple steps toward building the power and the freedom necessary to confidently and lovingly connect to people from all walks of life.

There is much knowledge in the minds and hearts of people. I have searched, discovered, observed, collected, and compiled the material in this book from years of experience. From that position, at times throughout the book, I indulge my arrogance not unlike the way someone who has won a race might, yet in no way is it intended to minimize your wisdom. From that understanding, I urge you to seek knowledge concerning connections and relationships so that you are able to overcome the absence of clear information in the complex cultures we live in. That absence of understanding is revealed in the absence of basic reasoning which helps us deal with connections and relationships both within the family structure and within educational systems. Experienced and informed parents seldom find the time to transfer their knowledge to their children in a coherent manner. When that attempt is made, it becomes an arduous chore for both parent and child. The information that does exist comes from well-intentioned but often misguided peers who believe, as I once did, that they already know how to play the game. These peers can barely help us with a handful of dance steps which teach us to manipulate relationships into manageable behavior.

     The adventure you're about to undertake will walk you through some simple steps and allow you to observe yourself closely and recreate yourself to the delight of your own eyes. Then you will graduate into the more intricate actions of looking at others—seeing inside their hearts and learning how to recognize the harmonic resonance which fuels the fire of passion that is latent in your soul. You will know how to heal the past and build the future, and you will find your First Love yet a second time around.
Undoubtedly, there are many different opinions on the topics covered in this manual. My intention is to offer alternatives and possibilities. From such understanding you will discover many more choices.

     You are welcome to write to me with comments about the ideas presented here. I will respond. The controversial elements you may find in reading this book should be viewed as introductions to things which should be discussed honestly, openly, and boldly among those concerned with such social ideas. Learning and exploring how to manage loving connections, I suspect, is almost anyone's concern.

How complete can this work be?

There is always a better, clearer, more direct, more eloquent, and more persuasive way of saying things. Often a writer delays a publication because of his desire or belief that he must produce a work that transcends time. He feels he has to create a work that is complete and perfect in whatever sense he envisions it should be. If I delayed writing or publishing for those reasons, my book would never be available to anyone. Wisdom and truth are not absolute subjects about which a final volume could be written. I view this text as a growing, building, and living organism and, as such, it has to be born. Since its original electronic release in 1999, this work has grown to an extent sufficient to survive on its own merits. If the reader discovers even a small truth that he or she finds valuable and useful, it will have satisfied my personal reasons for writing it.

I bring forth this child to you. I offer these words to you, that you may build your own wisdom beyond where mine can take you.

Don't be deceived by the simplicity of the presentation. There are many important issues brought to light in this manual which will awaken your thinking and give you confidence in your own wisdom to live fearlessly. I will teach you how to find new paths and new people along them and, with this new wisdom, take Love to the next level.

My Dear Niece . . .

I began this book from a collection of letters between my sweet young niece and I. Often you will see dialogue which is spoken to a particular person. Such dialogues are the way I spoke to her. As I spoke to her then, I speak to you now. Choosing to read this book is an act of friendship and it shows the vibrancy of your passion to live. Therefore, I intimately dedicate my communication to you.

I have shown the earlier articles from these writings to many women. Many have insisted that I speak to women, all women, rather than just a young woman, or a wise woman, or a brilliant woman. As time went on, others expressed a stronger interest in the earlier collection of essays, which had already been growing. Many have earnestly asked for more, insisting that I should cover a broader scope than the originally expressed intention of addressing younger woman. So I expanded the view to include all women.

However, it became clear that large portions of the materials on emotions, actions, manners, marriage, and many aspects of relationships are quite readily applicable to everyone and would provide greater flexibility of judgment in managing loving connections of any kind.

The topic is universal and therefore has to speak to the broader realm of connections and relationships of the human person. Therefore I again broadened the scope, while ultimately retaining a slant towards strengthening women's particular perspectives and interests, from the very young to the wise, mature woman. The writings grew to become my personal book to you, each one of you.

What if they read this book?

"Uncle, you're writing me a book of tricks to catch a boy? What if he reads it? He'll know I'm working him." You might suspect that a book like this would give details of intricate strategies and tactics of conquest. Then you will say to yourself, "Ah! They will know my strategy."

That it is definitely not the case. If they read this book, they'll know where you are coming from; they will understand better how to relate not only to you, but also to themselves and others as well and they will display a lot more respect for you.

If he thinks you are applying the information in this book with him or to him and thinks you're manipulating him, you only need remind him that the thrust of the book is openness, honesty, and the elimination of devious manipulation. He'll realize that you're for real and are being honest, since that's what I'm suggesting is the greatest tool you have. I'm giving you some tools to make it easier for you to be honest and to allow yourself to come out as a complete person. You've not deceived him by knowing and applying the things you learn here. In fact, it would be useful to have him read this book as well for his own success in his relationship with you. I do not know of any current textbooks where all this information is together in one place.

During the past several years I have reviewed about thirty or more titles wherein one might have expected to find at least some of the information contained here. I saw most of these titles as earnest attempts with good advice which could be used successfully. In contrast with that, the current work reaches beyond sets of rules or explanations of clinical observations and intrudes into the laboratory of everyday life. This book seeks to provide and teach independent and honest thinking. I believe this can be achieved through the options and alternatives presented here without a judgment of value given to weigh ideas in favor of my ideological preferences, but to entice, or even force the reader to examine them and determine what options he or she will choose based on his or her own observation and understanding.

The information provided in these pages may help provide a standard approach and establish commonly understood principles in the creation and maintenance of connections and relationships. It can create an underlying point of departure on a given course and contribute to a reduction of friction caused by too many different, rigid, or unknown values.

Emergency first-aid-kit

Let us assume you came to me for advice right in the middle of an ongoing relationship crisis for which you demand some quick solutions. Prompted by your urgency, I will sweep, in this section, through the items of pressing importance and broad applicability to resolve some of those pressing questions, even without the immediate benefit of other preparatory steps covered later in the book. Understanding the following elements and considering them in your actions will provide you with a relative level of comfort in most instances. As with a first aid kit, you probably do not need all its contents right now; therefore, feel free to scan quickly and find the pertinent points.

1. As a means of keeping your mental attitude relatively peaceful you must keep it in a comfortable state. To do this, I urge you to begin this simple meditation immediately: Listen to your breath. Simply sit in a comfortable space, eyes closed, and do nothing else but listen to your breath.

After you have done this a few times and find it easy to do, add this new step: Observe your environment with your heart. This is done imagining that mental or physical space around you is getting larger and larger in all directions, and noticing whatever is in that space. In other words, get the idea of the space around you and imagine stretching that space, and observe whatever appears in that space. Don't attempt to analyze it or figure out what it is or is not. It's an observation drill. Apply innocent curiosity, the curiosity of an infant, who looks at a new object without opinions. The infant simply observes and notices objects and looks at them with curiosity, and becomes conscious of them, without logical understanding, without wondering why or why not. It's the first stage of understanding. It is simply being aware of a perception. Don't complicate it by adding things to it to make it more interesting.

You should spend from 10 to 45 minutes per day on these two steps exercise as a regular practice.

2.All of life seems to become more delightful when approached in a spirit of exploration and innocent curiosity with the desire of making new discoveries and with the willingness to have things turn in a completely opposite way than you had wished for. This attitude prepares your mind for the losses, which are unavoidable, though they're only among the many parts in the whole scheme of things. And they are temporary. Your ability to experience losses without becoming irreversibly devastated will often open channels to higher degree of pleasure and ecstasy. The deeper the pain and sorrow you can experience with equanimity (evenness of spirit), the higher will be the ecstasies and pleasures you can and will experience. Life is to be experienced completely, with all its highs and lows. If you do not open your heart to loss, you are not opening your heart to the possibility of new love. There's much to be gained from love lost. There is nothing to be gained from being frozen in the fear of lost love.

3.The secret of making your dreams come true has to do with the mental readiness to have them happen. What you experience today began with thoughts and fantasies and was made real by your actions. This is something you will have to learn from experience and you will know which of your wishes are ready to materialize and when. In general, making your wish come true is subject to personal beliefs and concepts of reality, all of which can be changed. But changing these things is in itself often a difficult task. It requires much time and dedication. You must dedicate yourself to any task (whether it is the conquest of a lover or a job or a class assignment) with complete intention and attention and treat the task as if it were the only thing you will do your entire life. This means that you give all your attention, effort and intention to the task. Doing anything halfway produces little if anything worthwhile and ends up a waste of time. Dedicate a certain amount of time to a project or an activity based on how important it is to you, remembering that there are many other parts to life. Nothing needs to consume you entirely, but during the time you have allotted to that project or activity, do give it your all.

4.Life is not a bunch of separate, independent pieces. All its parts and colors are closely knit into one large panorama of seamless existence. Therefore, understanding one small part of it alone is not enough to assume that one is living a complete life, not to mention a fulfilled one. As you move through the book, you will find ample opportunities to experience how people's lives, thoughts and activities are interlaced with the, livesand of others. All parts of existence are relate.

5.When a channel is open, it flows in both directions. Read this three times! This means a couple of things. First, if you feel something in connection with another, it is almost certain that they have a similar feeling. Minimally, it means that something is happening on the other side, with the other person. What actions they will take depend on the social constraints they apply to themselves and on their personal beliefs.

The emergency kit is brief. It will help as a temporary, quick fix. Start this very day to do this simple exercise. The results will pleasantly surprise you.

Beyond this first aid kit, this book advances through logical progressions, of a likely path for the creation of meaningful connections. A cursory review of the table of contents will give you a fair idea of that progression. The sections and chapter titles are self-explanatory and do not require any additional introduction.

Chapter One Once Upon A Time

and practices) can be defined as a union of any group of people into a family, legally sanctioned by the authority of civil, religious, common, or other laws. At various times in history this has included monogamy (a sexual pair, usually male and female), polygamy (a man with wives or concubines), polyandry (a woman with husbands or several male sexual partners), and other less acknowledged marital or family arrangements, including those of the same gender.

Part I
The Fairy Tale

Once in awhile,
Right in the middle of an ordinary life,
Love gives us a fairy tale.

~Anonymous ~

Chapter One
Once Upon A Time

A high school student wrote an essay, "Snow White in Black and White" from which she allowed me to borrow a few paragraphs:

"Once upon a time there was a girl who had everything that she ever wanted. She had a good family and good car and was entering a perfect relationship with an attractive guy.

"Life was good! Then her parents told her that they were getting a divorce. The next year her loving husband wrecked her beautiful car on the way to see his mistress.

"She does have some major problems, but the biggest problem is the psychological war that is going on in her head. She has talked herself into the idea that her parents will get back together, that her husband will discover that he loves her more, and their marriage will develop into the romance they once had.

"Every girl dreams of a Prince Charming to come and sweep her off her feet, but what happens when her lover doesn't come? What happens to the girl? Psychologically the only thing most girls know is that they must not settle for anything but the best; to settle only for a fairy tale ending."

This excerpt illustrates the youth's keen awareness of both worlds—the world of fairy tales she grew up with and the real world of sorrows, disappointments, and not so disappointing routines.

She continues:

"We expect our marriages and relationships to be long-running fairy tales and when they're not, instead of examining our expectations, we switch partners and try again to live our dreams."

There is an almost cynical flavor to her attitude and expression. Is she speaking of the irony of the circumstances in her own life and family, or is she referring to her expectations of it?

The profound truth in her last statement might, today, amaze even her. In a subtle way, however, she too continues to entertain the hope that if a fairy tale ending cannot be had, she must pour coal into the boiler of an engine that she hopes will still be able to run. She faintly suggests that if we cannot have the fairy tale, we can at least try to salvage its pieces and build some kind of structure that will in some way convert the fairy tale into whatever lesser, but tolerable, relationship.

The Fairy Tale Phase is a time filled with wondrous dreams of fairy-tale-love-stories-come-true and last until the dawning of the social reality expressed and understood by our young writer. New worlds have become visible now. She begins to mourn the ending of the Cinderella years when her life is visited by her parents impending divorce. She wrote her essay many years earlier. Had she ever imagined her black and white world would come to bring gray into her own life?

Her dreams are not lost. Only their appearance will change and she will learn how to create her life in new ways in the years to come. Thus, a driving force behind the materials in this book is: to acquire and exercise the ability and willingness to re-examine one's expectations.

What we are about to learn in this manual is how to harness the power of the heart and with our minds, create the nest upon which it dwells, in order to give ourselves the ability to create our dreams.

Historical Review - Marriage and Social Economics - Gender Stereotyping

Understanding why things were done in the past empowers us to change our lives and our futures. Without that understanding, we can go on forever doing things just because they were always done that way. It as often been said that failure to know and understand the past condemns us to repeat it mindlessly. Hidden, unknown and/or misunderstood reasons for past failures are the principal reasons we repeat those failures, not only on a social scale but also at the individual level. Let's review the background on courtship and marriage systems that is prevalent in our social structures. An understanding of these traditions will give you a better perspective on your overall approach.

Marriage (including in our definition historical concepts and practices) can be defined as a union of any group of people into a family, legally sanctioned by the authority of civil, religious, common, or other laws. At various times in history this has included monogamy (a sexual pair, usually male and female), polygamy (a man with wives or concubines), polyandry (a woman with husbands or several male sexual partners), and other less acknowledged marital or family arrangements, including those of the same gender.

Christianity is the self-admitted influence to the elimination of all other forms of marriage except monogamy:

"The progress of the race toward monogamy, as well as toward a purer monogamy, during the last two thousand years, owes more to the influence of Christianity than to all other forces combined. Christianity has not only abolished or diminished polyandry and polygamy among the savage and barbarous peoples which it has converted. But it has preserved Europe from the polygamous civilization of Mohammedanism, has kept before the eyes of the more enlightened peoples the ideal of an unadulterated monogamy, and has given to the world its highest conception of the equality that should exist between the two parties in the marriage relation. And its influence on behalf of monogamy has extended, and continues to extend, far beyond the confines of those countries that call themselves Christian." (Catholic Encyclopedia, History of Marriage.)

For a long time the responsibility for the creation and arrangement of marriages, regardless of type, fell upon the parents, who used to make all arrangement. This process was driven by the parental need to take care of all the social and economic needs within the family's concept of their status in life. These needs were very valid to ensure the well-being and future security of the family and the children. This process functioned during periods in history when life didn't change much from day to day. People normally lived in one small area of the planet their entire lives; their emotional constitutions did not change much from year to year.

The roles of men and women were very clearly defined, and there was such a wide agreement to the system that it was taken for granted as the appropriate method, and therefore never questioned. The idea of love played little or no part at all in this process. The prevalent thinking was that love was something that would develop over time within marriages and tightly woven families. Love didn't enter as a consideration for the social contract of marriage. If it developed at all within the marriage, love would have been a fortuitous bonus to make that social contract more palatable. I'm talking about the substance of the contract as function of legal responsibilities. Thus I'm excluding those components which do not require legal sanction nor are mandatory, such as the gatherings, outings, holiday feasts, and similar activities.

If we never bothered to look at historical precedents, we would still be able to speculate the outcome of events taking place within our present observation and we would be relatively accurate, realizing as well that these outcomes demand change of the core of the social fabric.

The Influence of Social Economics

Arranged marriages are still a time-honored tradition is some cultures. They were practiced in Europe to a marked extent, but not as extensively in the Americas, as the European cultures moved there from their lands of origin. However, what remained of the tradition also underwent further change in the entire Western world.

Chapter One — Once Upon A Time

As the agricultural economic systems began to change and began to be replaced by mass processing, we entered the Industrial Revolution, which affected much of the western world at first and later the rest of the world. Men left their homes to work in places often too distant from their families; consequently they were unable to be the supportive pillars they had once been. After the beginning of the Industrial Revolution, family roles began to blur. Women inherited roles men were no longer fulfilling within the home, given that men were not there to execute them.

Men continued to hold a dominant role; whether traditional or not, that dominance seemed to have been taken for granted so much so as to be believed natural. Yet men had to make concessions under these new settings. These concessions can be generalized in terms of greater freedom to women, still within the traditional structure, which appeared to retain some rigidity with regard to tightly defined roles and behavior.

Men defined themselves in very strict social terms with very precise ideals concerning masculine behavior, emotional responses, mental outlook and socioeconomic roles. Men were supposed to be strong, to take punishment or adversity without showing stress. They were not supposed to cry or show any emotions or weaknesses. (Some of these attitudes continue today. We have generally been raised to associate women with weakness and we chide men for showing weakness by calling them names associated with feminine characteristics.)

These role definitions seemed to work for a while; but the 20th century was to be one of extraordinary economic change, which forced other family and social changes.

Wars added stress to tradition. Boys were gone to the front. Their parents were not in a position to exercise their traditional roles, much less enforce them long distance. Those who left often married abroad; or when they did come back, their betrothed had gone to other men; planned arrangements didn't materialize. Families were scattered throughout the planet to escape the scourges of international disasters.

Transition of Roles and Stereotypes

Social economic needs and religious and civil laws changed the nature of marriage, yet gender characteristics were slower in changing.

Consider the belief structure in men of the first half of the 20th century and look at standards such as those already mentioned. A man does not cry or show pain. He controls his family and his woman. He has the last word. Women's conditioning on the other hand, so long as they accepted or displayed some semblance of subservience, did not receive any serious attention. Not a great deal was done to structure her behavior beyond external appearances. The superiority assumed by men made them arrogant. They did not feel the need to understand women, never mind being bothered with regulating their emotional training. In fact, the standards applied to men were a convenient separator, not only of roles, but also of the standards that came to be thought of as characteristic differences of the sexes.

These differences were in fact learned patterns and not gender characteristics. Women, not as emotionally restricted as men (it was okay for women to cry, show emotions, and be impractical), were free to develop in areas where men had neither an interest nor an understanding. This lack of understanding in men resulted in the arrogance of his supposed natural superiority.

The feminine development created the characteristics in women that men found hard to understand. In fact, the feminine focus of development was a way for a woman to elevate herself to the height or higher than a man. She could become more emotionally stable; and she did (purely a value judgment on my part, based on the fact and observation that unregulated emotional development usually allows greater emotional stability). She had a stronger constitution for work and was able to endure things men would never encounter in their workplaces. (I have witnessed, even in the latter part of the 20th century, that women work longer and harder in enough instances to justify this generality.)

The more liberal education of women (in the sense of freedom of focus or direction) allowed them to achieve the emotional and social powers which finally brought about the feminist revolution. Suddenly women were in a world where they could demand their rightful position at a man's side, in war as well as in business.

This battle continues and it has not yet accomplished all that it should accomplish for women with regards to the higher concept of equality purportedly championed by Christianity at the beginning of the millennium. What is important for young people to understand is that we are still living in a volatile period of transition and the contemplation of relationships must be viewed with a combination of concepts in mind.

The traditional paternal concerns were for the welfare and economic security of one's children. But there was another concern which came to be significant: the durability of the family. The family breakup rate during mid to late 20th century compared to the latter part of the 19th and first part of the 20th centuries is staggering.

These destabilizations of personal security and fast changing social and cultural standards demand, in addition to considering economic and social aspects with regard to the formation of relationships as well as personal security, that one look at oneself as an important source of personal stability through an understanding of self, without which no viable existence can be achieved, let alone promote the establishment of viable relationships.

You don't love a woman because she's beautiful,
She is beautiful because you love her.
~ Anonymous ~

Chapter Two
Fast Forward

When we are clearly aware that we are living through continual social changes, personal needs are difficult to view in a predictable fashion; therefore, it becomes important to attempt to project from current situations into the future. In other words, based on the direction we see things going, where are they likely to be at any time in the future?

Even after Christianity succeeded in eliminating all forms of marriages except monogamy, the process of establishing relationships continued through the tradition of betrothals. A betrothal represented a commitment to marry at some predictable time. Going steady is not the same thing and does not represent a commitment to marry. Whether or not betrothals will result in marriages is rarely predictable these days.

If the traditional betrothal practices were unworkable, if only because they would simply not be practiced, we can guess what type of practice would have replaced the tradition: Modern men and women had to take on the job of finding mates for themselves and all attendant responsibilities of making the proper selection, taking into consideration some of the things parents would have naturally taken into account in the past, such as financial and social status.

We could imagine, rationally so, that parents at one time would have taken extreme care in evaluating any number of potential husbands for their daughter(s), such as checking a suitor's social status, family history and living conditions and working out agreements with the groom's family. This is a truly complex transaction.

Are the young people in our culture in a position to be capable of such a selection process? If you, like many others, are not, let's get you prepared. But this shall not be just a preparation for marriage. It is a strategy which you will find helpful in understanding and therefore creating, the necessary social and intimate connections which will contribute to a reasonably pleasant existence.

Lessons From Traditions

When the practice of elders and parents choosing mates for their children was abandoned in our culture, the reasoning and responsibilities that had been the realm of parents and elders was not transferred to the children. Parents still feel responsible for the welfare of their children in many ways. Therefore, it is natural that they attempt to exercise some degree of control over their children's choices of friends and connections. It is rational that you consider your parents' and elders' thoughts and feelings in these matters.
It doesn't mean you have to accept their judgment blindly. You must insist on clear explanations about their feelings and consider them when making your choices, especially in the matter of the marriage contract. It is a contract, and the advice of parents and elders is usually based on experience worth drawing from.

Failure to consider advise from the people who love you and who have experience is uncomfortable for everyone and tends cause elders to inject a subtle rejection of the budding connection; this makes for a shaky beginning. The value of such advice will become clearer as you continue reading and begin to consider the complexities of marriage presented in later sections.

Modern Complexities

Life evolves into ever more complex organisms. This statement personalizes life and attributes to it the ability to have a goal or a purpose beyond mere human species, applicable on a broader sphere. Applying that concept to social evolution, it would be rational to extrapolate the path of human evolution from the simpler, smaller family units and tribes into larger family units and communities which would necessarily have to change to accommodate planetary social, economic and political shifts. What I call modern civilization is a term that cannot be used to refer to or to visualize all cultures. The lifestyles of many countries are much different from the western world. Many civilizations exist just as they have for centuries.

In this book I deal primarily with modern civilizations in the western countries of the planet and their social practices. However, many aspects of interrelations on a human-to-human level (for example, the emotional level) presented here are applicable and deserve consideration in understanding those elements in other civilizations.

You should be able to see, with a little research into the works of other sociologists, or through personal observation of almost any modern social group, that we are moving through major social transitions. The complexities of intermixing cultures and shifting moral, ethical, and social considerations are visible everywhere. For a young person who has little with which to compare, this transition might not be apparent, except in his or her observation of the variety of lifestyles among peers.

Since the beginning of mass education, the responsibility of teaching love, family, relationships and sex seemed to have transferred from the parents and family to an ambiguous and undefined educational system. Thus, this whole sector of wisdom has fallen on the uninformed lap of youth itself. The teaching of creation, management and nourishment of relationships and connections seems currently to be in the hands of school peers--the older ones transferring their beliefs and ideas to the younger ones. This has opened the door to a school culture of sexual and social behavior which in itself is one of the principal barriers to successful connections, in particular and often to success in other areas of life.

The cultural differences in these volatile times are, no doubt, becoming more apparent to you every day. The dating, courting, and methods of establishing and maintaining connections are so extremely wide ranging that it would be a very difficult task to detail it, explain it, and suggest modifications for more effective methods.

Socially acceptable behavior differs to a greater or lesser degree in each particular locality. The result is a set of vague, un-inspected values everywhere. Youth, not having some clear guidance along these paths, tends to learn the culture from peers, usually older ones, and usually without wisdom and understanding.

The only consistency across these values are the platitudes carried by mass media and mass entertainment, which, while appearing profound and fresh, do not provide meaningful uniformity, to the point where no two people can completely agree on the meanings of words like love, commitment, honesty, openness, loyalty, betrayal, and others.

The resulting confusion manifests something like this: A young girl, who was crushed throughout her school years because, on dates, she refused to have sex, thinks there was something wrong with her for passing up such opportunities. Such an experience is the result of subtle, unwritten rules of the school and surrounding culture.

Remember some of these peer-generated rules?

"You are a prude if you don't kiss on a date."
"You are not 'kewl' if you are still a virgin after age 16."
"If a boy doesn't call you the day after a date, then he doesn't like you."
"If he doesn't ask to kiss you, he doesn't like you."
"If he doesn't try to touch you sexually, he doesn't think you are beautiful."
"If you refuse to let him touch you, you're not with it."
"If you don't have a steady there's something wrong with you."

Chapter Two — Fast Forward

"If you call him, you're showing him you like him too much and you will drive him away."
And the list goes on and on.

"The option is to be a loner in school; it can be safer than the intrigue, gossip, and heartaches!" told me one youth. This inadequate environment is the furnace where the nature of our youth's future connections is forged! From it we get dubious courtships practices:

Look, for example, at the latter part of the 20th century, where we consider ourselves relatively progressive in the ways in which we approach relationships. One method of developing relationships is predominant amongst youth and adults alike. It is the practice of concentrating a few years on a single individual; and after failing that, the practice is repeated over and over until hopefully one individual will be the right one.

Time is one of the factors that force this trend. In most people's experience, there is not enough time to develop solid, lasting connections, much less to develop the many other necessary connections vital to one's growth and understanding of relationships. The connections that develop tend to be random and accidental, usually occurring as a byproduct in the process of fulfilling other obligations, like work or school.

Finding oneself in an accidental connection becomes a convenience that breeds complacency, wherein rudimentary needs are satisfied. To safeguard this relationship of convenience, one restricts his or herself from a genuine effort in finding and developing the type of connections he or she might have originally desired. The apparently unspoken and unwritten agreement of exclusivity simply does not allow for the creation of other the type of connection the person would have really sought, had there been time for it.

These arrangements create an artificial scarcity of connections,which after a time can result in obsession or anxiety about connections, and finally a feeling of inadequacy. The individual begins to wonder if there is something wrong, which is making it nearly impossible to make more diverse connections. This is compounded by peer pressure which says it is socially unacceptable not to have somebody.

Following this need for connection is the latching to the first person one meets. This type of connection, again, fills certain basic requisites such as desire, the appearance of having someone, a sensual reaction in the body, and some degree of being overwhelmed by the physical appearance of another. If the feelings are not mutual, it becomes a game of conquest to the one with the greater need. Reacting to his need, the one who feels unwanted begins to undertake tactics and strategies to motivate the other person toward a stronger connection. If the conquest succeeds, it then begins the repetitive cycle which varies in duration, eighteen months, two years, five years, seven, and so on. The cycles described above are illustrations of what has been observed with reasonable frequency.

The natural resistance to change adds to the problem. A person may find oneself in a relationship for whatever personal reason. The daily activities of work and all other pressures of daily existence make it difficult to break the cycle and one continues in the same manner for years, nearly incapable of changing anything. Eventually one begins to believe oneself inadequate. Overcoming the feeling of inadequacy once it has acquired is one of the most difficult situations anyone can encounter. Perhaps one of these connections progresses into a marriage.

When you look at marriage as it has evolved over the years, you will notice that social and personal needs are not explicitly part of modern arrangements, so all that is left is a social contract for the upbringing of offspring. The rest of the necessary ingredients in marriage, such as the mutual emotional support of both partner's needs, is entirely unpredictable.

That alone makes marriage, as currently established, inadequate as the only type of social intimate relationship. Even in the presence of the marriage contract, key contractual elements of the union are easily violated, particularly after the contract has been terminated. Such violations include lack of child support, and post marital assistance to the mother for her transition to an unmarried state, especially if she is burdened with children for whom she must provide stability during their growth years.

Marriage as it is practiced in modern western cultures has become somewhat inadequate as the only viable social unit or structure for connectivity and union. There are also the complications of cultural, religious, and social diversities within relatively small geographical regions. It is abundantly clear that the high instability of the marriage warrants inspection not only of the marriage system, but the contemplation and introduction of new systems of connections and relationships.

Rarely a single day goes by without my being told intimate details by a man who is emotionally empty, or a woman burdened for many years on her own, with little or no support, either economic or emotional, all because of a broken relationship. It's not rare to find married men and women who are helplessly bound to dissatisfying relationships, at best.
These are broad and sweeping statements. But for individuals drawn to this book in search of guidance, those inadequacies are vivid personal experiences: the breakup of a marriage, a betrayal of loving promises. Lacking that personal experience, statistics reflecting these problems are not hard to find, if only derived from personal observation of the high rate of broken marriages and broken connections.

I make frequent use of the word connection as a more encompassing concept to intentionally blur the traditional term relationship with a more adequate word to include the variety of ties to other members of the society. Such usage is necessary because in our day we not only have to consider the obligations of a traditional marriage connection and responsibility to children, but also our personal and emotional needs throughout life. We must also consider how a smooth transition is achieved from one area of social and economic responsibility and status to another, without destroying our

personal well-being or the well-being of those around us.
So what path is there for young or seasoned individuals, or anyone who wishes to build or reconstruct his or her life to attain some success with intimate connections? There are new love-ways.

Chapter Two *Fast Forward*

Only love let's us see normal things
In an extraordinary way.
~ Anonymous ~

Chapter Three
New Ways To Love

Customs and traditions exist because a degree of consensus has been achieved within a social order as to what constitutes rational and viable behavior. The individual looks at customs and traditions to help him decide proper conduct. At the same time, we also admire the dreamers and mavericks and the heroes who have the courage to stand up against customs and traditions; their rebellion turns the tides of traditions into new ways of life. Today's customs were yesterday's rebellions which proposed and brought new solutions to vital problems. Today's problems will yield the solutions that will produce tomorrow's traditions. Sometimes traditions and customs no longer answer today's needs. Yet, it is difficult, if not impossible, to open new doors to experience and knowledge without upgrading learned ideas, habits and traditional realities that in fact have closed those doors.

You may already realize that some customs, traditions, unwritten rules, conventional wisdom and what everybody knows are no longer valid or applicable. Why, then, even after you've separated from those that advanced traditions you no longer hold valid, and after you have made your own personal advances, do you continue to apply these rules that you no longer believe in? Why are they so difficult to change, even when you want to and think you should change them? The reasons and resolutions are found through self-discovery.

Self-discovery and self-improvement are necessary ingredients for success in many areas of life, and are significantly important in the creation and maintenance of connections and relationships, including friendships. Your measure of success, of course, is relative to the achievements of your personal objectives. This makes it vital, not just a good idea, to acquire a clear understanding of yourself and a clear sense of your personal objectives. Understanding your personal objectives is imperative. Often, acquiring clear objectives is a process of development which continues throughout your lifetime. Nevertheless, at any given moment it is possible to be aware that you are taking actions guided by some impulse, even if you think or believe you have no real clear objective. In other words, something is moving you to do what you are doing at any particular time.

Set your mind at peace, re-discover and upgrade your concepts of self, and re-discover and upgrade your reality and understand how it affects your life. Establish new and realistic objectives for all the parts of your life, including what you need, want, and can give to your connections to others. What you don't know about yourself will continue to enslave you.

Setting Your Mind at Peace

The first action of self-discovery requires at least some minor mental and spiritual preparation. That is the purpose of the meditations. Many people find it useful to engage in daily meditation. It is not only useful, but also vital. I recommend at least fifteen minutes each day. If you find that the exercises I present here are not as in-depth as you desire, you can determine what type of meditation is best for you by reading up on the subject. There are thousands of books and seminars to choose from. I will just give you a favorite for its simplicity and surprising effectiveness in clearing the mind, helping to relax and contemplate life or anything of your interest, particularly for self-discovery.

"Listen to your breathing" is my favorite. It is a deceptively simple and effective meditation. Sit quietly, and simply pay attention to your breathing. Of course, often there will be thoughts coming in, and all kinds of feelings and ideas.

Do not make any effort to try to get rid of them. Allow them to flow, and maintain as much of your attention as possible on your breathing. Whatever feelings, anxieties, anguish or emotions you sense during this exercise, simply allow them to flow through; don't resist them. Occasionally you might experience fear. If this should happen, simply experience it. Do not attempt to do anything with it or to it. Do not attempt to stop it or push it or change it. Experience it. Notice what it feels like. Observe it with curious innocence, as if you were doing a scientific experiment. If you feel panic while doing this, don't panic! Experience it with the same curiosity and amusement. This attitude helps you overcome your natural instinct to resist or avoid fear or pain or other discomforts.

No matter what happens, simply experience it. If you keep it this simple, it will be a powerful tool in resolving many fears and obstacles, in reexamining preconceived ideas; and you will discover many truths.

Any variation of an activity that allows you to focus gently on a rhythm, and which is comfortable for you, will accomplish the purpose of this drill quite well. Some prefer to listen to the rushing water of a brook. Others like the waves of the ocean or recorded sounds of the womb. The idea is to find a peaceful rhythm.

Self Discovery

You are who you think you are. Everything that you think, and all the actions you take can only come from your sense of who you think you are, whether real or imagined. When you change your mind about that, your thoughts and actions will also change. How did you get here? Experience, decisions, conclusions, determinations, indoctrinations, conditioning, beliefs, perceptions, survival needs and thoughts are some of the major elements that make up what today you see as You. You are a fairly defined processing and generating system, with perceptions and filters to limit certain perceptions.

At any point in life, one usually has, on one hand, a relatively firm foundation of these components quite stable sometimes to the point of rigidity; and, on the other hand, areas that are somewhat always under development. All of this is who you are. It is what others see as you, modified by their observation system, which is part of who they are! What is visible to others is a physical form, an energy emanating entity.

Let's slant our focus more directly on aspects that deal more directly with your contact with others.

When you find a mutual attraction, or affinity, often thought of as chemistry, what is taking place is that the energy emanations (electrical, magnetic, or other) blend into what can be called harmonic resonance; a form of natural attraction of harmonic energy.

Once we have a working idea of who we are, we can review the impressions we make, first on ourselves, then on others. How we perceive ourselves is more important than how others perceive us, and can affect how others perceive us. We all make an immediate impression on others. What we think and believe and how we feel about ourselves is part of what emanates from us, and it strongly affects how others perceive and feel about us, even through their filters.

The assessment that follows will help you develop a clear image of yourself, if you find it otherwise difficult to establish who you are by direct observation of self.

People with whom you associate are often very similar to you, and you might notice how over time you begin to take on each other's mannerisms and characteristics. For example, if you're not very expressive, either through words or other body signals, it's usual that people who find you compatible will, just like yourself, find it difficult to be expressive.

There will be people who are likely to find you acceptable and attractive just as you are right now. It should be of little concern if you don't attract people that are popular or seem to get all the attention. (If they're that popular, they might not be able to give you the attention you want, anyway, having to divide their attention amongst their fans!)

If you feel you want to change, consider what attracts attention and whether that is what you would like to have as an attribute or characteristic. Some characteristics might be good and useful, others, not so!

There is no need to embark on a deep study of self to understand who and what you are now. This is an ongoing process. Your immediate awareness of yourself and who or what that appears to be right now is a matter of immediate concern.

To help you acquire a clearer idea of who you are now, try this simple exercise.

Reality Readjustment Exercise

After you are fairly accustomed to the meditation above, add to the practice the following exercise:
1. Make a list that answers some of these questions:
Considering all the things I do, what am I mainly trying to obtain as an underlying purpose for all my actions?
What are some of my habits?
What kind of emotions do I experience more frequently?
What things make me really happy?
What kind of activity do I enjoy best?
What are some of the things I would like to change about myself?
What image do I think I project about myself to others?
What aspects of my behavior bring people like me, close to me?

You can make a longer list if these questions are not thorough enough. The purpose is to make a simple assessment of yourself which allows you to inspect your own impressions of yourself, which in turn gives you the opportunity to change some of those things that you might want to change. If any items come up in the above list with which you don't feel comfortable, and where you still experience conflict, and would like more immediate change, do the next step of the drill around that idea.

It will work well to help you review and re-evaluate ideas, beliefs, customs and traditions, that somehow seem to be a barrier to your success.

2. Make a list of as many of these learned ideas, customs, traditions and beliefs, including and/or specifically concerning dating and relationships, (if you want to focus on that) as you can remember, including those you really think are good ideas that work well for you. (This can be done on any subject of interest, as well as the items from the first list in this section. Making this list will help you achieve meaningful change in all of these areas.)

3. Once you have completed it, go down the list in any order that interests you, and test each item separately by considering the following:

* Where did I ever get this idea?
* Where have I seen this take place?
* Who did I admire or love from whom I accepted the idea?
* Mentally review the conversation in which the idea was first presented to you, and how you came to accept it as true.
* How can this idea be true?
* How can it not be true?
* How did my life work because I applied this idea?
* Was I persuaded into this by someone influential and simply accepted it without inspection?
* Do I have a special interest for it to be this way?
* Would I lose something if I discover this to be true (or false)?
* Allow yourself the same respect or love that you held for the person that gave you the idea in the first place.
* Review the idea in the present and decide anew whether it's a valid idea or not, and allow yourself to create a new idea if you need one.

There is a deceptive simplicity to these steps, which may make you think, "Oh, this wont work for me." But if you apply these simple steps, even after having done only a partial list and applied it to at least one important idea, you will see an immediate adjustment in your way of thinking toward a greater confidence and comfort in your ideas and beliefs.

We often have ideas that we've carried with us for years, taking them for granted as truths. Individuals of extreme influence in our lives have given these ideas to us. We have totally accepted these them as truths. When your present observation suggests that such ideas may be inaccurate, yet you cannot change your mind about them, it is useful to attempt to try to recover the moment you were convinced the idea was true. You want the precise moment you made the decision to accept the idea(s). This drill helps you locate those moments.

The drill should be done lightly and quickly, in five to ten minutes. It can be repeated again and again whenever you encounter reality conflicts that don't resolve easily with brief contemplation.

If you find it difficult to stay focused in the drill or are not able to guide yourself without getting distracted, you can sit with a trusted friend, and work on the drill together, where you are asked you the questions, and helped to answer them. You can also elicit the help of counselor who has an understanding of how to deal with deep exploration of the mind. If you don't get immediate results within five to ten minutes, you will have at least set the machinery in motion, which will often continue to unravel conflicts on a subconscious level.

Some of us who have lived a bit longer can be insidiously trapped in our old codes and beliefs, taking for granted that they are the law of nature, becoming quite off-handed in dismissing any possibility that new idea or belief can replace those codes. An interesting and common example is the idea of betrayal and the personal injury incurred from it, and the fixed meanings a betrayed person can carry that gives him or her, an unworkable and distorted reality.

Let's say a relationship came apart because she had sex with someone else. He feels something is wrong with him. and is humiliated. He knows what his peers will think of him for allowing such a thing to occur, and dreads the confrontation. He now thinks her action means she doesn't love him. He thinks, "She would have been stoned to death for such behavior in some ancient culture! How dare, she!"

I'm not taking a moral stance here. I'm simply pointing out how codes can be ingrained into the mind in such a way that no new ideas could possibly be allowed to enter. By applying the reality adjustment exercise to those concepts, a person will be able to adjust his/her reality to a more rational, personal stance. Unless you are willing to do some serious rethinking, the drill above will not do very much to allow you any flexibility with deeply ingrained ideas.

Once the idea is reviewed with this drill, your own change of reality, the new compassion, empathy, understanding, and forgiveness will often affect the other person by helping them break their pattern of betrayals.

Loneliness - Individuality and Separateness

Toward the middle of the 20th century and shortly thereafter, strong social movements advocated the concepts of individualism, which has remained with us late into the 20th century. It emphasizes individuality, which in practice frequently translates into isolation. It was understood as, doing your own thing, creating yourself, becoming personally independent of the social values of the time and establishing your own values. In theory, this was a worthwhile concept. It appeared to mark the end of the era of A Nation of Sheep, (by William J. Lederer). Then, it appeared as if people were easily deceived and had a propensity for conformity. Although the book is generally a political essay, it did speak of a social system of calculated mass deception. The following decade gave us the illusion that such trend was at an end with the birth of various social revolutions.

Yet, the concept of individuality and personal independence was broadly misunderstood and served many in their escape from personal and social responsibilities to peers and others with whom they would naturally come in contact. Becoming independent meant focusing on one's own interests to the exclusion of the needs of (and duties to) others. The concept was taken up by the advertising trade and became a recurring slogan, in multiple variations. Be a notch above the crowds! Let your individuality show! Be independent! And of course, the more material items you acquired, the higher your social status. Its impact grows even more apparent at the end of the 20th century.

The sheep were led into becoming irresponsible, egotistical and, above all, socially separated and lonely because they were now indoctrinated on how to be individual and independent.

Individuality also implies rejection of authority. Paradoxically, while most people we run into assert their differences and individuality, their actions are highly conformist to their own concepts of social acceptability.

The independence of this dubious individuality has translated into irresponsibility, that is, inability or refusal to respond intelligently to situations. Being independent and being irresponsible are not synonymous. Yes, do think independently. Inspect information and evaluate what you observe, but do not let that isolate you and give you the false idea that you're not responsible for what is going on around you. It is imperative that you take those around you into consideration when you are moving the conclusions of your observations into action. The golden rule is alive: Love thy neighbor!

The Hidden, Dark Self

Nothing restricts a person's rise and growth as the ignorance of his dark side. What is the dark side? The debate of good versus evil will continue to rage in our societies no doubt, till the end of time. For a practical application here, let me make a couple of statements about right/wrong, good/evil. We usually accept as wrong or evil those things which are considered evil by the group, usually believed harmful to the group. On a more personal level, we tend to accept that selfish actions, which harm others, are wrong, and generous acts, which benefit others, are right. Since our actions and the things that affect us are based on those beliefs, we need not at this time explore any deeper meaning in these concepts.

Until a few months ago I had only a vague sense of this aspect of our humanity and of its impact on our lives. Then, I stumbled across Michael Parson's work on "Trance-forming Your Dark Side," and it provided me with a form of expression that lent a high degree of clarity to what I subtly understood. There is an aspect that is applicable in the context of establishing and building connections; and that is, "underlying motivation." When I reviewed my own actions in this light I discovered that it was very easy to hide my own deeper motives from myself, and present to others more plausible reasons for proposing a relationship.

Here are some lucidly interesting examples that can be found to be rather common.

The outward expression is, "I like you, you are beautiful and have such a great personality, and I am tremendously attracted to you." The underlying motive is, "I am afraid to be alone, and I will say anything to get anyone to connect to me, so I can avoid the pain of being alone."

Outward expression: "I admire your ability and your intelligence. You are an unusual person, and I believe we are meant for each other." Internally, "You are wealthy, and my connecting to you will finally free me from the daily worry of having to survive, not knowing where my next meal will come from, or whether I will have enough resources to keep a roof over my head."

This is what has come to produce the cliché, "getting together for the wrong reasons."

It is important that we become aware of our deeper motives in our approach to relationships, and that we make these motives clear to others, at least prior to making any long term commitment, because otherwise these motives will act as the undisclosed information which may ultimately destroy the connection.

It is true and often perhaps even necessary that we consider our own desires and needs when establishing a connection. In this way we can say to the other, "While my own personal motives have to do with my own personal gratification of my sexual needs and the avoidance of the pain of loneliness, I propose to give you ever-so-much more that I will ever take from you, as well as support your own deeper personal, emotional, and self gratifying desires." Then focus your actions in the relationship to provide the other with the things they need with a priority above your own personal needs. That is the only way you will receive beyond what you ever needed or hoped for.

That is using your dark side energy toward what will ultimately benefit the other person as well as you, rather than ignoring or hiding or repressing your dark side; for to do so, is guaranteeing failure.

In addition to looking at your own motivations, addressing your dark side is a fruitful exploration that can give you more insight on discovering some of your dark aspects. These aspects are the things you find distasteful in others. You may not need to work on this aspect immediately. However, every time you find yourself annoyed or feel a situation has gotten out of control as a result of distasteful actions of others, the first path to resolution is to review your own characteristics and habits and notice what you find in yourself which is very similar to the actions or motivations of another who has presented a problem to you.

People do things that we find unpleasant at times. Our own reaction to those actions can give us a hint to elements in our dark side that are the same or similar. Here is a very vivid example: A child breaks an object intentionally. Parent A works with the child to clean up the mess, and then with a compassionate attitude tries to communicate and understand the problem which prompted the child into that behavior. Parent B becomes enraged, punishes the child, and attempts to control the child into 'correct behavior' through one kind of force or another. Parent B is likely to have aspects in his own dark side that are similar to the child's dark side. That parent would do well to ask himself, "When I did similar things as a child, what were my underlying motives? What similar characteristics do I have at present, where I would do something unpleasant toward another? What reasons have I used? If I would set reasons and justifications aside, what are my real motives?

If one cannot look at these things on one's own, one might want to find a trusted person to help her/him review them in conversation.

Discovering and redirecting the energies of one's dark side is an on-going process. Review these aspects as frequently as necessary, particularly when you are having unusual difficulty in resolving situations.

Ready for Action

Regardless of your personal condition, you have to carry on with life. With that in mind, it's best to constantly work on self-improvement as a routine activity. Life circumstances don't wait until you finish your training. They take place when they do.

No matter how many times you read and re-read strategies and tactics about any activity in life, your personal state of mind or condition is the major, most influential factor to the outcome of your undertakings. You can spend a lot of time figuring out which is the best way to approach a situation, and have the best logical solution, but if you are not in a relatively healthy mental and emotional state, your success is at risk.

To ensure that your state of mind remains healthy and that your emotional state is cheerful and relatively peaceful, do your daily meditation and the self-discovery drills in this chapter.

I know from training thousands of people that only reading about a skill is not enough to learn it. It requires remembering to do it, and practicing it. I have found that repeated exposure to information is a very workable method of moving the information from the thought stage into the action stage; repeating the action many times will convert it into a habit.

Doing daily meditation and working on the various exercises, taking exclusive, undisturbed time to dedicate to your personal improvement and comfort is must. There will come a time when you will have only your own wisdom to draw from because, having attended all the masters, you will have become one. You should make it your personal mission to carry yourself beyond what is already known; extend the development of human ability by your own desire, intention and dedication to move past whatever you read in these pages, or beyond whatever any master will have ever told you. This way, you will remain ready for action at all times.

In summary, your mental and spiritual state and communication skills can be a thermometer, which tell how ready for action you are. The more you understand these aspects of yourself, the more effective you will be in creating the outcome you desire.

Rules?

The most important objective throughout this book is to help you achieve the ability to exercise your own judgment and have a comfortable degree of certainty, rather than set rules of behavior.

Evaluations of behavior, that is to say, explaining or translating the actions of people to a tentative meaning of intentions, are educated estimates. A wide spectrum of experience and exposure to different cultures and different realities, and a profound understanding of human mentality and spirituality, can arm anyone with a relatively accurate ability to predict life events.

Consequently, single-minded, rigid rules, while possibly valid as a teaching tool for the novice, have no real value when judgment is engaged in trying to understand what is going on around us, and deciding on things to do.

A heart that loves is always young.
~ A Greek Proverb ~

Chapter Four
Meeting People

In our social settings there are few openly acknowledged events or places specifically designed for people to simply meet and relate with others. As it is becomes clear this is a vital part of social interaction, such places and events are beginning to sprout for that purpose.

There was a time when public meetings and socials specifically designed to bring people together were commonplace. I am reminded of the stories an elderly aunt related to me about the town square meetings, where men and women would form rows, men on one side, women on the other, and they would walk by each other and present themselves, so all could see all. The adults already had certain arrangements in mind. They would watch carefully to see what types of attractions would form, and make further arrangements accordingly. These socials were vital to the harmonious development of the community.

Today, we don't have such pointedly focused events. Meeting people is incidental to activities such as school and work, and in nightclubs where the music is usually too overwhelming to allow proper introductions. In our society today, young people have been forced to devise ways to expand their connections by looking for alternative methods of meeting people.

Where Do I meet People? Anywhere! It takes developing a style and a method of action with which you are comfortable. There are always opportunities to meet people. No need to ignore them or be shy about becoming aware of places to meet. Restaurants, shopping plazas, supermarkets, in sum, anywhere and everywhere.

The Internet

Today we are blessed (or some would argue, cursed) with a tool that transcends or seems to transcend barriers of time and space: the Internet. Setting aside technical aspects of it, let's quickly view the possibilities of this medium.

In spite of what some people may think, the Internet is an unusually good training ground for exercising and practicing one's ability to communicate, and to develop a wide perspective on what humans are like. In addition to being the largest library on the planet, filled with almost infinite resources, the Internet is a force that is changing our culture, the face of which shall be unrecognizable from one decade to the next.

Among these vital elements are the chat systems, the message systems, news groups, and other similar systems for the communication between individuals on a personal and often intimate level. These tools put us in contact with millions of people across the planet and we have at our fingertips more potential contacts and connections in a shorter time than we ever dreamed possible.

Through the Internet, there are millions of people seeking to make connections with others of like minds and similar cultures and ideas. It is a fruitful ground for gaining practice at meeting strangers and being able to communicate on simple to very complex subjects. If for no other reason, you might want to consider utilizing this resource to practice learning to communicate—to learn about many different types of people and how complex and interesting they can be.

And there is no shame in connecting romantically on the Internet, as long as you are sufficiently cautious! When you meet this way, you are meeting people who know your mind before they know you physically, which can be a very powerful thing. You are also under no obligation to meet on a physical level if you are not completely comfortable doing so. It is not a good idea to give out information that makes you immediately more accessible. If you have made a connection that you feel is strong enough to warrant a physical meeting, make sure you agree on a public place, and don't present yourself unless you are sure this is someone you can trust, and with whom you wish to continue to communicate.

When you broaden your horizons and meet people on the Internet, you will begin to understand certain aspects of connections that were never before envisioned. You have at your disposal a means to end the scarcity of possibilities in finding your special someone. You will find more and more people who are truly special in so many different ways. With this awareness, you can approach the matter of connections with a great deal more confidence, and without the traditional pressures of scarcity.

I wonder if there was a time when the telephone was loved and despised in the same way that the Internet is today. The Internet has been called the antichrist and the perdition of society, while simultaneously being hailed as the greatest invention of all time. On the desktop of your living room, you have access to a world full of life and love. It is a unique world. It is a valid source of communication. The Internet is a truly vital environment. Don't make the mistake of minimizing the value of the connections made through this medium. There is life there. There are real people. It's an enlarged community, and the people you touch and connect to are real. Approach this medium wisely. It's a slice of the very social environment where you live your physical life, only faster. It contains the same dangers and opportunities as your day-to-day business and social life; but because it's so easy to reach across vast distances, it takes place at a faster speed, and the dangers and opportunities take place in a shorter span of time.

Dating And Personal Services

This method of meeting people consists of organizations which have a database of clients who, upon paying a fee, entering their personal data and sometimes creating videotapes for viewing by other members, are encouraged to meet other members. Dating services are a valid and viable method of reaching beyond your immediate circle of acquaintances, and often will produce pleasantly surprising results. Any stigma attached to persons using such services is unjustified. If your circle of acquaintances is not an adequate source of connections, by all means, don't be afraid to use a dating service. These days there are relatively inexpensive services on the Internet. They provide the additional advantage of quick response time, so many of the basic elements people wish to discover about one another can be reviewed in a short time.

Repeated Exposure

In the process of meeting people, there is an important aspect that will raise your possibilities of success. This is applicable whether you have made an initial contact or not. It is the concept of repeated exposures. Repeated exposures will bring you more solidly into the consciousness of others, and finally you will become part of their reality. It is a known and recognized principle that repeated exposure to something creates the reality of that something. Without much effort, you simply create exposure. So it makes sense to establish patterns of repeated exposure to the types of people you are interested in meeting. Find places which you would not mind frequenting at regular and repeated intervals. This pattern will pay off in the end, since other people also tend to follow patterns of this kind.

The advantage of this method is that once you've been seen in a place several times, people will feel more comfortable about coming to greet you and to talk to you.

There is also a long-term usefulness to the process of repeated contacts. For example, let's say you are interested in establishing a connection with someone who doesn't seem to show any interest at first sight. What would be a reasonable method of creating an interest in the mind of the other person? The most workable method is repeated contact. This contact begins with the initial greetings and a repeated series of other gentle social contacts. Careful observation will allow you to understand what interests the other person.

This observation takes place routinely. It is always interesting to watch people do things. What are their needs, habits, and interests? People, whenever possible, dedicate more time to those things that bring them pleasure; they talk about the things that interest them. They may also discuss matters that others bring up, but this is easy to distinguish from the subjects that truly interest them. Once you understand some of these things, you can gradually increase communications, showing interest in some of the same things. Now, this interest has to be genuine. If it is not, they will see it as false. Of course, you have to be aware that your interest in other people is based on more than the initial attraction of their physical appearance. Otherwise you will find it difficult to express a genuine interest in things which generally did not have any importance to you.

It is a fair certainty that this process of repeated contact and communication will develop into a more meaningful connection if there is really a coincidence of interests.

Priming a Connection - Staying in Touch

The activity of meeting people is fraught with all kinds of fears and apprehensions. Now, even though you are past the meeting stage with your new connection, and have become part of his/her reality, it is important that you continue to look at this stage as an area for development of your contact skills. You must take action and practice your skills. This process is often called flirting.

1. Flirting is a way of testing the water without getting drenched. It's the royal mating dance of our species, and it allows a gradual unmasking and revelation of intimate aspects in the comfort of lightheartedness, and pleasant communication.

First, your instinct to call was good. Communication is generally more productive than absence of it. Now, to add power to this you have to pay attention to some important points: Have a clear idea of what you want to communicate. You did have something to say; you wanted to invite him out. He turned you down. Asking was not your error; not allowing him enough time for him to make it happen was. You should have paged him early enough to allow him to respond without any pressure. To accomplish that it would have been wise to leave him a message saying precisely what you wanted: "I called you to invite you out on Saturday evening. Please get back to me to let me know if you are available or would want to plan alternatives, if you like."

That is a clear message. Additionally, since it is left on a message system, he is not under pressure to respond instantly, and will have a chance to think about it. To demand an immediate response could result in a negative one.

If you've not really had a chance to engage in spontaneous communication in meeting people, you may get flustered when talking to the other person, either directly or when leaving messages. So it is important that you practice saying the message. It may also help to write it down and say it aloud until it's easy and comfortable to say. This may make you more confident and you will not feel quite so awkward and uncomfortable. This may seem silly, but it is helpful, and it works.
Remember that sometimes people will turn you down because they themselves don't know how to respond, and out of their own frustration they may stumble and end up saying something they didn't really want to say. So it is best not to put the other person on the spot by forcing them to come out with quick or spontaneous response.

If you are talking to him on the phone and you sense that he is in a rush, it is better to simply cut the message short and tell him, "I see you're in a hurry to go off somewhere. I guess this is not a good time. Will you call me when you are more comfortable and less rushed, say later tonight?"
This avoids the meaningless chatter and the embarrassment of catching him at a bad time, with no readily available way to end the conversation.

In recommending that you practice what to say and do, I'm not suggesting you develop an act which does not truly represent who you are. Even an act cannot truly hide who you really are if you are trying to deceive. In recommending practice I hope to help you develop and deploy who you really are so the real self will not be hidden by embarrassment, shyness or other inhibitions.

The message here is to be real in observing and following logical approaches to respond to your observation.

Manageable Circle of Acquaintances

Available time and attention limits how many connections one can acquire and nurture. First, realize that connections must be created and recreated, and time must be dedicated to their maintenance. Keeping this in mind, we know a manageable number of connections would be limited. Most likely they would be arranged somewhat in concentric circles consisting of a small group of intimate connections at the core, with larger, less intimate connections in each of the next outer circles.

Here we are not especially concerned with what might become the core group of intimate connections. I don't think it makes sense to simply call out a number, but experience shows that a wide circle of acquaintances is desirable and comfortable for most people. An important reason for developing a broad field of connections is that it alleviates or eliminates the sense of scarcity of friendships that many experience because of their social or professional settings. After meeting, repeated exposures, and a sense of reality of those you want within your circle of acquaintance you can develop important intimate connections. That becomes a fertile ground for love. Even love at first sight cannot happen if there isn't a fairly broad and manageable circle of acquaintances.

Love is that condition in which
The happiness of another person
Is essential to your own.
~ Robert A. Heinlein, Stranger in a Strange Land ~

Chapter Five
Love At First Sight

As far back as I can remember, I have observed that we seem to give special meaning to "love at first sight" as the seed for the most incredibly passionate, all-consuming connection we could ever have. I won't conclude from this observation that love at first sight is universal and happens everywhere to everyone. I can state that it is significantly prevalent and visible in many societies with which I have come in contact.

I remember when I began to feel these strange sensations inside my body at the sight of certain people. It is interesting to note that the spark of the "love at first sight" fire doesn't necessarily relate exclusively to members of the opposite sex. In some countries, boys and girls are segregated at an early age. It is also observable that children go through a period of distaste for the opposite sex. Within this framework this powerful sensation can be triggered at the sight of a person of the same sex.

Nothing has been more baffling to young and old than this fire called love at first sight which has long been, and continues to be, the underlying theme of some of the world's greatest literature and art. Countless songs, plays, poems, and all forms of art have been created in reference to first love. Undoubtedly this is one of the most powerful impulses of life. Love at first sight is an irresistible, nearly uncontrollable feeling within the heart and mind of humans. Much discussion and argument surrounds this phenomenon. Interestingly, especially as we mature, the extent depending on our social surroundings, we are very often urged to control this desire, to resist it, reject it. Stifling these feelings—this instant love—results in an accumulation of inner conflict and distress.

Yet, when we are young, this impulse is the driving force that launches us into a relationship, and eventually causes us to change our way of life, if not our very nature. We change ourselves and change the way we do things; we take more responsible jobs, and we even move to other far-off places on the planet in pursuit of love.

What is behind this force of love at first sight? It has often been associated as a purely sexual reaction of the young. Yet, the young will tell you it is most definitely true love. They tell you it is something beyond mere lust. There are strong reactions in the body, but we know there are many things that accompany it.

Another unexpected revelation about this force is that we can see it in full bloom not only in the hearts of the young, but delighting folks well into mid and late life. There is something more important about this force, and it cannot simply be dismissed. This force is a fire must be understood, kindled and nurtured. It is the fire of life.

To most people this is the most memorable romance in their lives. From that point on, nothing is or can ever be as good. Or is it?

The mind can be trained, the heart only restrained. So one can attempt to combine into a connection both the elements of the heart and the things that the mind dictates, but giving the heart the benefit of the doubt often makes us ignore the dictates of the mind.

When the heart engine is running, there's little recourse but to try to drive it safely; there's no stopping it. So you have to understand a few things about this emotion.

The experience is usually unexpected. It seems to be turned on by something external hitting a trigger within. It can continue to run for a long time or it can stop as unexpectedly as it turned on. You must develop the ability to manage your personality, style of being, and thinking in such a way that you use the power of this energy to enhance your life, not to run it into the ground. This means combining without restraint the power of the heart, and the nest upon which it lives and thrives—the mental and physical environment that the mind must create.

For a moment, imagine this scenario: Someone you are instantly attracted to has just walked through the door. You are struck by a bolt of lightning and suddenly find yourself floating on a cloud. Your eyes meet and suddenly something strikes you deep inside. You find yourself experiencing a strange desire and your heart is pounding faster and harder. You don't recognize it as routine desire, like the desire for something delicious or an attractive garment. But it should be clear to you that it is indeed a desire, because the thought of not making a connection and not coming to know this person on a deeper level can actually feel painful.

You also know that it was like a meeting of the soul; but there is another sensation that you will rarely acknowledge, and that is the sexual aspect of the desire. It is a desire, and it is a sexual desire. How can we assume the feeling is accompanied by a sexual desire? You can see the answer to this question if you simply consider the idea of maintaining this connection without an eventual sexual contact.

The thought of not achieving a sexual connection a deep sense of loss will invade your whole body. It becomes evident from other sensations inside you that you are experiencing a sexual desire. You will feel in the body sensations in erotic regions, whether the stomach, the chest, or solar plexus (most common) where the butterflies live. It doesn't matter where the sensations manifest in you. You are most definitely feeling a strong sexual desire. Don't be embarrassed that this feeling surfaces and can overwhelm you. I'm not emphasizing sex with the intent to prove its greater importance, but to prevent you from denying its existence. A real connection takes place on all planes of existence—mind, body, and soul. To attempt to deny or separate the sensual feelings as if they were not part of the experience, or as if they did not belong in that experience, will bring you a great deal of anguish.

The Reciprocity of Passion

An Open Channel Flows in Both Directions: This means what it implies. If a true connection has taken place, that connection is the passageway through which feelings, emotions and sensations will flow in both directions. Let's say you are a woman and we were discussing the feelings you might have for a man towards whom you felt an instant attraction. Often you wonder what he felt when you looked at each other. I assure you, as one who has been there and knows, whether he ever admits it or not, he has in fact experienced sensations almost identical to yours. Keeping this in mind, there are certain things you can expect.

He will figure out a way to make contact with you. You will begin to focus on him, as he will now focus on you. You will be drawn toward each other and a meeting will most likely take place.

You experienced this and within a week he asks you out (or you ask him out), and then again the following week. The passion and interest are high. This is the best time to engage in much communication, from the trivial to the sublime. This is when the iron is hot. Your physical person vibrates with desire, but you often don't act upon your physical desires during this period. Don't worry, there is nothing lost. Often you have to allow things to settle down a bit to recover from the intensity of the desire.

This is a good pausing point to review your emotions, illusions and the reality of the situation.
Emotions and Illusions

Self discovery leads to self development and expansion. Your success in life in general, and in connections in particular, requires a keen awareness of self—your own objectives, your own mission—even if your mission is adventure and discovery. This awareness of self becomes a necessity in establishing connections because in the estimation of a connection you must clearly see where your emotions lead you, what the reality of the situation is for others around you, and finally, what your illusions are.

Chapter Five — Love at First Sight

The process from thought concept to reality, which may be part of the various stages of development, begins with thought and turns to imagination or fantasy, and then to illusion, strong desire, verbalization and writing, a broadening agreement with others, and eventually ends with the actual manifestation in the physical realm. Therefore, illusions themselves are not a problem, provided you are aware of what those around you see as their reality. If you attempt to move a connection into your illusions you will become disappointed when the person withdraws, stunned by the unreality being forced into his consciousness. When that happens, you may find your illusion taking the place of your reality in an effort to assert it as real, and you will feel your world caving in and your heart filled with obsession.

Pay attention to the realities others communicate. Our societies are so incredibly diverse and complex that it can be quite dangerous to assume that everyone around you needs and wants the same things you do. Sometimes that is the case, but more often it is not.

This is especially important when intimate personal objectives are discussed. You should know your own objectives, and you should quickly discover the objectives of others that come close to you. When these objectives are not in some way closely related, it is a certainty that the two of you will not travel on the same path, and it is unlikely that there will ever be a merging point. There is neither need nor can it bring you success to cause others to deviate from their objectives. Nor is there any value in attempting to change your own inner direction to accommodate someone else's objective. This will shrink you as a person and you will waste your time at best.

Once you have sorted out your emotions and illusions, the task is to recreate the initial fire if it has diminished. That is the reason why, if the connection didn't strengthen quickly, it will be in excess of a month before you might hear from him. But you probably will. If you feel comfortable calling him, by all means, do so. He might just be hoping you will!

Male and female characteristics and their sizing and measuring are almost a ritual, which is sufficiently distinct as to merit identifying and labeling. This stage deals with physical and mental confrontations and dances that allow people to observe each other's humanity, sexuality, mental aptitudes and social status.

Part II
Posturing and Positioning

I only wish to be the fountain of love
From which you drink,
Every drop promising eternal passion.
~ Author Unknown~

Chapter Six
Beauty and The Beast

Appearances. This is one area of life where people get very little training.

Ugh! He's so ugly. He wears braces; he's fat; he's skinny; his teeth are crooked. There are thousands of negative reactions to the appearances of other people, and they are totally irrational. Beyond general cleanliness, the reasons we immediately dislike or do not feel attracted to others are a serious accumulation of personal inadequacies—a severely distorted sense of reality of what beauty is. People project what they don't like to see in themselves onto others. This is more often than not the reason people find others ugly or unacceptable.

The idea of presenting an acceptable image is a rational concept, but only to the extent that one does not present an image that is offensive to another's traditionally acceptable protocol of introductions and manners. Beyond that, and once a more open communication has been established, carrying the acceptable image to the point of hiding one's true self is the initial seed of the downgrading of oneself in our social setting.

This predominantly affects women more than men, who believe they do not fit the right look, particularly in appearance of the body.

You've been watching television and browsing magazine images where everyone is airbrushed to the advertising world's standard of beauty. You have heard your peers talk about this person or that person being gorgeous, and you want to be sure your guy fits their standard of gorgeous.

People are trained and conditioned with these ideas. You have been conditioned to believe this is what beauty is. You believe it because you have been inundated with the images since before you can remember. Your model of an acceptable look becomes extremely limited. As a result you end up with few possibilities because you are eliminating people based on your comparison of what they look like to the images your mind has been conditioned to believe they should fit. The men in the advertising ivory tower huddle to establish their idea of what a woman should look like, and they impose on women in a very subtle way, a false standard, and they buy into the idea. This is widespread nonsense. When a woman accepts that viewpoint, she is contributing to an unnatural separation based on sex and appearance. Women have been practically forced into accepting appearance standards which are restrictive and nearly impossible to reach. They are forever striving to reach these standards, while their male counterparts are traveling along the roads of power.

When a woman has fallen into the trap of believing herself less beautiful, less intelligent, less capable, less entitled than her male counterpart, she has accepted the conditioning, and is now moving along with the herd of sheep to the sheering and the fleecing grounds.

Happiness is usually felt when things are going well in our lives; things seem to be going our way. We are accomplishing things that we set out to accomplish. Our loved ones usually support us in those ideas.

Having a body like advertising models has little to do with life accomplishments and happiness. Attempting to have a body like it can become a thankless task, since it's a myth attainable by only a small number of people. As an unattainable goal, it gives many women a sense of failure. This failure translates into lowered self-esteem and dissatisfaction with self. Having a body that conforms to the advertising business does not guarantee happiness.

We've heard a thousand times that beauty is in the eye of the beholder. Yet, we repeatedly fall into thinking that there are certain standards of beauty without which we are automatically handicapped. Nothing is further from the truth. If you continue to accept that you are less acceptable because you don't meet the standards imposed upon you by irrational social pressures, you've allowed the seeds of subjugation to germinate. Subjugation is becoming a slave to another's will or ideas. This will cost you in peace of mind that will undermine your physical and emotional health for years to come.

A girl or woman who thinks she does not meet acceptable standards of appearance, and there are many who think so, even when she realizes how she has acquired such ideas, finds it nearly impossible to recognize that she's not only perfectly acceptable, but outright beautiful.

We always hear "beauty is only skin deep," and a whole number of other clichés. Yet, women continue to feel self conscious about their appearance. Well, beauty is not only skin-deep. Beauty emanates from the soul and radiates through the mind and through the body. If you don't feel beauty arising from within, it will never shine through you.

Let's look at some of the standards for beauty with which we are raised. We are bombarded with images of what is considered beautiful by the media. These are usually European-American people with symmetrically proportioned faces; very slender, emaciated waifs, or curvaceous females with large breasts and tiny wastes, men with washboard stomachs and muscles that make them look as though they spend all their time working out, and black men and women with light skin and European features. People exposed to these images from childhood are trapped into this concept of reality. The trick is in the manipulation of ideas through a very simple method of creating realities. Reality is more frequently acquired through exposure.

A more natural reaction to another's appearance, if they do no meet the standard, might result in any number of rejecting attitudes which are reactions to the unknown or unfamiliar. When the natural rejection of the unknown is compounded by indoctrination and brainwashing that reinforces it, the problem is enlarged significantly. It becomes the first seed upon which other, more dangerous rejections are built and trained upon, such as racial, social, and professional bigotry.

If you think you are not beautiful because you do not meet certain standards, be well aware that you have been brainwashed. You have been deceived into thinking you are not acceptable unless you strive for and meet those standards. Brainwashing can be a difficult mental condition to resolve, and may require many hours of counseling. If you think you have serious problems related to your appearance, it will be useful to get professional counseling. Knowing by what means you have been brainwashed will help you begin to dispel the idea that there is something wrong with your body.

The first indication of brainwashing stems from the fact that the person suffering from it is utterly unable to shift even slightly from the idea that there is something terribly wrong with her appearance. Part of the difficulty comes from the hidden source of the brainwashing. One may think it is personal decision. That is not the case. The most difficult ideas to change are those which have not been acquired through our intellectual reasoning and personal choice, but which we have been conditioned into believing or accepting, usually through social repetition.

Should everyone simply like everyone else? Theoretically, this is not as far fetched as one might imagine. However, let's just talk about removing some of the unreasonable restrictions of what is acceptable, because that can become so limited that you experience nothing but scarcity in your connections. The following drills will be quite effective in correcting the acquired false perceptions discussed above.

A Remedy to the Beast

If you feel you suffer from scarcity of beautiful people in your life, then I would like to expand your horizons so that you will see that there is a lot more beauty in the people around you than you have been led to believe. It is important to adopt a way of discharging your repulsion or rejection of people you don't at first consider beautiful. After you do the following exercise you will come to see the obvious; there is nothing really wrong with them. The remedy is Observation.

If you find yourself disliking the appearance of too many people, you should start by simply looking at the features you find undesirable in them. If you are embarrassed to look at them, you must then find some way of observing them; for so long as you find them distasteful you will remain a slave to these unknown dislikes, and your ability to relate to people will be tremendously impaired.

You might try to acquire a picture of the person to observe, and simply look at the elements you think you find distasteful. This exercise will remove much of the reaction toward the unfamiliar and the ugly. This is done by simply observing the image for a sufficiently long period of time that you begin to notice that you are no longer repelled by it. That is all! Miraculous! Minimally, this will increase the acceptable appearance range in your mind. While you are observing someone to rid yourself of the idea that she/he is not attractive, you might appear to be rudely staring. However, looking with interest and staring are quite different. There is a certain detachment, almost a disapproval connected with staring. Whereas interested and approving observation is easily acceptable. If you find someone looking at you and smiling, it may be embarrassing, but not as distasteful as staring is likely to be. Be careful that you are not offensive.

Why is this practice important? Aside from needing a large field of potential connections, you also have to be a compassionate human who is accepting of others. You simply must be able to relate to others, regardless of their supposed physical inadequacies.

The acceptability of things around you depends primarily on you. Acceptability is not a quality of an object but a judgment on the part of the observer. Your attitude and upbringing make them so. The more things you find distasteful and repugnant, the narrower will be your field of vision, and

you will lose much of what there is to experience in life
Finally, this drill is not workable by simply knowing it. You must do it. It is vital to expand your ability to see life in all its aspects, which will in turn help you grow in wisdom, intelligence and compassion.

A Remedy to the Beast in Beauty

You may have run into this problem of your appearance in the self-discovery section, depending on the depth with which you approached it. If you still feel shy or unhappy with your appearance, do the drill that follows.

This exercise will take you a long way toward a realization of self value, as well as help you realize the beauty that has been hidden within you. Here again the remedy is Observation.

The drill is simple and it is done about five to ten minutes a day for as long as you find unacceptable features in your body. Stand naked in front of a mirror and observe your entire body. In the first phase of this drill, look for those features you find distasteful in others. See if you can find any of those features in your own body. Observe each feature for as long as you can. Watch your own reaction to the observation. Simply observe the physical feature and observe what happens inside you while you are observing.

Now do the second phase. A slight change in perception. Sometimes you may see something in others that you don't notice in yourself; thus you are being asked to look outside first. In the second phase, you find the features you consider unacceptable in yourself that you didn't already see in the first phase. Observe these features and watch your reactions, just as you did in the first phase.

As you do this over time, you will notice that, little by little, those features, which started out as being unacceptable, are now quite acceptable, and often beautiful. When you have done this exercise honestly every day for at least a few weeks, you will understand that beauty emanates from the way you think about yourself and from what is in your soul. The drill is finished when you can embrace and be pleased with the way you look.

Some of the most beautiful women in the world do not meet the Advertising Street standard of beauty—not by a long shot. If you don't believe this, take a count of the people you admire and love and see if their appearance meets the beauty standards that you've been conditioned into applying to yourself. For the most part these are plain, common people who do not meet the gorgeous standards you have set for yourself.

Let me again emphasize that merely knowing that there is a drill is not enough. You actually must do it daily.

The way you feel about yourself transmits unequivocally to others. Others will see you as you see yourself. If you don't like yourself, it will hinder your prospects of having others like you. The drill will go a long way toward restoring what is truly there—your innate beauty.

After you have had some relief and success with the preceding exercise, if you are still unhappy with your appearance, you should do the Reality Adjustment exercise in the self-discovery section. Modify the questions to the topic of appearance and looks.

Here is an example. The first two questions in the Reality Adjustment exercise are:

* While considering all the things I do, what am I mainly trying to obtain as an underlying purpose for all my actions?

This question becomes: * Considering all the things I do with regards to my appearance, what am I mainly trying to obtain as an underlying purpose for my actions?

* What are some of my habits?

Change it this way:

* What are some of my habits with regards to my appearance?

Now, continue going through the questions, altering them to fit how you feel about your appearance. Do the exercise in earnest; don't simply read the questions. Write down your answers and think about them carefully.

A part of you has grown in me.
And so you see, it's you and me
Together forever and never apart,
Maybe in distance, but never in heart.
~ Anonymous ~

Chapter Seven
Exploring Emotions

In the process of developing and navigating through the emotional maze of a starting relationship, one experiences all types of emotions associated with the connection.

Here are some of the more common ones: cooling off, nervousness, feeling stupid, jealousy, betrayal, deception, nervousness, anguish.

Cooling off is where the intensity of the emotions or the attraction appears to have diminished. You may ask, "Where did I go wrong? I don't understand." You didn't go wrong anywhere. Remember that if what you had at the beginning is sensual/sexual electricity, the cooling off should come to you as no surprise. The initial sexual attraction is not always strong enough to keep a connection stable, particularly if it is not pursued through the continued stimulation of that same electricity. In order to strengthen the connection you must now pursue other avenues of communication.

Now let me bring you back to an idea that I pointed out to you at the beginning: What is your purpose? Because you seem to be slightly at a loss right now, as things have cooled a little, you may say, "My goal is to turn things around and show him who is really in the position to beg for my love."

Manipulation and punishment do not get you what will ultimately bring you happiness. Making him beg for love may be an interesting adventure to test your manipulative abilities, but it will end in nothing short of disaster, with you at the wounded end of it. Therefore, continue to focus on maintaining a lightweight social connection, and continue developing other areas of understanding in order to build and enhance the connection.

Nervousness comes from various things; one of which is your own fire and zeal of being attracted. You can do little about nervousness; however, it may lessen if you have what you want to say ready to deliver clearly. This will minimize the apprehension and embarrassment of the nervousness.

If he senses your nervousness, he will most likely attempt to make you feel comfortable. He will try to keep the conversation gentle and easy. If he doesn't notice that you are nervous, it doesn't matter. At the very least, you might make a mental note of the fact that he's not sensitive enough to notice your emotions.

You were nervous when you called him this evening, and he told you what he was planning, even before you asked. Then you asked him what he was doing! You thought you should not have asked? You're right; there was no point in asking him, because you had your answer. However, you still need to communicate what you wanted him to know, "I see you had other plans, I tried to get you earlier in the week, but unfortunately, I didn't leave any messages, so going out tonight is obviously out of the question! Ok! Enjoy your barbecue. We can get together some other time!"

Ensure that every time you are in contact with him he has a clear idea of what you want him to know about your thoughts and feelings. Having a clear idea of what those thoughts and feelings are ahead of time will go a long way toward lessening or eliminating any nervousness.

Feeling stupid may happen quite often, and the reason for this is the lack of experience and practice in communication. This feeling can be eliminated by the act of formulating a clear idea of your message and practicing the delivery before you make the call. But if you have made the call without thinking about what you are going to say, or you find that you are at a loss for words, a good way of opening the conversation might be something along these lines:

"Gee. I feel so silly that I called. I am even embarrassed to say why I called."

"I don't believe that between the moment I dialed the number and now, I forgot the reason I called."

"I feel strange because I don't really know why I called."

"I'm a bit embarrassed to admit I don't know why I called. I guess I just wanted to chat about things in general."

At this point, if he is sensitive enough, he should gently prompt you into opening up to him. No man will allow the conversation to end once he knows you have something to say, but are not saying it. If he does end the conversation without prompting you, then make a note of the fact that you are either not that high on his list, or he is likely insensitive to your emotions. There is also always a chance that he is just as uncomfortable as you are. With practice, you will be able to distinguish the meaning behind his words.

If you do find yourself feeling somewhat uncomfortable with these types of calls, it would be a good idea to keep some of these lines in mind and use them when you are suddenly at a loss for words. Eventually you will come up with your own spontaneous things that will make the conversation easier and more comfortable.

If the call progresses, say what is genuine, truthful, honest, and earnest. Say something about which you have a real concern or interest, not something you make up to fill silent spaces. It is better to have silence than meaningless chatter. If you are at a loss for words, you might want to pause and notice what's on your mind. It may simply be that you're somewhat satisfied that all your questions and concerns are satisfied for the moment, "Gee, I'm at a loss for words. I thought I had lots of questions, but you must have satisfied my curiosity entirely. I'm going to have to reconsider a few things. This might awaken some more questions or areas of interest."

"I'm totally pleased with all that you said; actually, your thinking is quite intelligent."

Never be afraid to praise when you feel it, but don't invent praise you don't mean. Let me repeat and make sure you understand this thoroughly: be real, honest, straightforward, and don't manipulate.

Manipulation with words can be quite annoying. Manipulation can be perceived as asking questions unrelated to what you really want to find out, but the answer to which will give you the information you're trying to extract secretly. In fact, you do not need to do this. Whenever you ask something you really want to know, it will usually be answered with more information than you asked for, so you will be able to understand the other person better, while being honest in your communication

Jealousy, betrayal, deception, apprehension and anguish can be disturbing, and they often work together in connection with some event or series of events.

Disturbing Emotions

Emotions are very important signals that you should learn to decode. By this, I mean, convert into something you can relate to and understand.
We generally perceive life as motion. We view it as path from one state of existence to another, perhaps endlessly. Objective is implied in that transition from state to state. In the human experience emotions are what the etymology of the word implies: outward movement. We think of it more as some form of internal energy that seems to take place in reaction to the perception that something significant is going on in an area of concern, which may require immediate corrective or defensive action, or simply a call to alert us of something unknown. An objective or goal forms a tension vector or line of mental force stretched between the present moment and the future. This emotion-energy impels one into action. In this case the individual generates the emotion at will, and not as a reaction to external stimuli.

The words we use to name various emotions are not truly descriptive of what each person will experience, therefore a prescription for how to deal with specific emotions is dubiously workable.

Chapter Seven — Exploring Emotions

Here I like to address what can be described as disturbing emotions, such as jealousy, anguish, apprehension, fear, anger, and other uncomfortable emotions.

It requires a bit of practice to sort out these disturbing emotions. Here are some quick ways to resolve the confusion, which, however, should not replace long-term work on yourself, your personality, and your metaphysical world.

Here is a drill or exercise you can do.

Imagine the worse possible thing that could happen in connection with the unexplainable emotion you feel. You will immediately experience a rush of energy through your body if what you imagine is what is actually happening or what may happen. When you become aware of the situation which is causing the apprehension, it will usually release in a rush of heat and/or other body reactions. Your may think that by doing this you will work yourself into an uncomfortable state; and you are not wrong. Why, then, do I suggest you do this?

The reason I am suggesting you imagine the worst is because imagining can help you release some of the potentially painful energy that you would likely come to experience if the situation were to become a reality. By mentally creating that situation (before it can happen), you will release the painful energy with greater ease. It is important to get that energy out of the way.

There is another element to consider here. It is possible and highly likely that the subconscious contemplation of the worst is, in fact, the source of the apprehension. By causing yourself to experience it before it happens, you will be releasing the pent-up energy connected to the potential undesirable event or situation. Then, if the event happens, you will not be crushed or surprised. You will have formed in your mind a safety net to deal with the difficulties. Having developed a mental tolerance for the least desirable occurrence will avert extreme instances of apprehension and anguish. On the other hand, if it turns out you were wrong, and it was not a signal of something bad, you will have been relieved of tensions which, in any event, prevent you from achieving your objectives.

On some level you did create this apprehension. The exercise doesn't make you create something that wasn't there in the first place, because in the exercise you are creating or imagining an event that contains the emotion which you are already experiencing. Placing the unpleasant emotion in the context of an event very often makes it easier to relieve it.

In addition to the drills suggested here, you can also apply the drills recommended for decoding perceptions to deal with disturbing emotions.

Decoding Your Perceptions & Emotions

Reality is the beliefs, ideas and things we have confidence exist. We trust that what we see and perceive is reality. Our reality is based on what we perceive. We believe there are ways by which we receive information, in addition to the physical senses.

The idea that there are other means of perception beyond the senses of the body is not a new one. I'm not going to explain, analyze, or categorize them, but I will share with you some interesting observations.

You've heard that sometimes when a person has lost the use of one of his senses, somehow he begins to develop other means of perception to compensate for the loss. Blind persons are particularly noted for developing other ways of sensing.

At one point we talked about the Internet. It is interesting to note that, in general, you have access to many people, but you normally communicate with typed words.

The absence of some senses to participate in the communications creates the urge to know what is not being perceived. I've talked to many people, and invariably find that most do develop other senses to perceive things about people they "talk" to on the Internet. I also have experimented with this medium extensively, and I can tell you there are many things to be discovered about the ability to extend one's perceptions beyond the senses of the body.

In order to understand your perceptions and the im-

Chapter Seven — Exploring Emotions

portance of the information they bring, here are some things that can be done.

When I was a young man in my mid 20's, I was beginning to recognize where these things came from. Once, I was lying in bed in another city, on a job. Suddenly I felt an acute anxiety. I immediately got an image that my daughter was doing something of which I sensed she did not think I would approve.

I called her. It was difficult to find her. That was a break in the communication channel, apparently purely coincidental to events beyond our control. Yet that was a signal that something was wrong. (When it becomes impossible to reach someone through the usual channels, you should make a mental note, and review later, as a matter of potential concern.)

When I finally reached her, she was with a man, and in all innocence told me she was just playing chess. I had no alternative but to accept what she said. It wasn't until a few months later that she confessed that it had been the very evening I called her, when she had contemplated this other man with desire, and the one she would now move toward. What she was doing or had decided to do was unclear, and hidden; thus it was perceived as an apprehension I sensed inside my body, triggered by something taking place at a distance.

Is it possible for anyone to experience what I felt at that moment? We all have the capability to sense such things. Notice feelings and images you get from your experiences, until you can distinctly establish which feeling is which. When that is clear, look for patterns connected to how the circumstances involved with such feelings or images take place. Notice what events take place before and after you have those feelings, images, or perceptions.

Once you see the patterns, you will be able to predict the perception and the reasons for it. This is how you can begin to learn to decode your feelings in terms of what they can help you understand and predict.

For example, you notice a certain sensation, feeling, or

thought which seems to come at random, and which seems to be completely disconnected from your current activity. When you begin to pay attention to this perception, you begin to learn to distinguish it from other types of perceptions. You can now start paying attention to events in the physical environment to see if you can detect a connection to a type of event. If you do discover such a connection, you will have a confirming feeling each time. Eventually you will be able to see the pattern, if there is one, and after a while you'll be able to find the perception increasingly reliable.

The process of being able to read and understand your feelings, perceptions and apprehensions, and resolving them, is a matter of practice. You must have courage to watch yourself and what happens. Trust yourself to recognize these energies and what they represent.

Manipulation, Secrecy and Lies

Nothing destroys a man or your connection to him faster than the discovery that he has been manipulated. This manifests itself in many ways, and you should take care not to do it. First, let me explain what manipulation is:

Manipulation is arranging your communication in such a way that you leave the other person no other choice but the one you offer. Manipulation is not itself a bad or evil. The word derives from mani = hand (Latin), and plere = to fill or full (Latin), by extension, managing with the hand. Manage skillfully something to produce a desired result. It has also come to mean, to mold a person into a certain behavior.

The word alone contains the idea that manipulation of another person is always undesirable: We understand from experience that, even if we were caused to do something we ultimately enjoyed, we sometimes found ourselves resenting having been walked into it without our knowledge about where we were being taken. Manipulation is causing others to do something they had no intention or desire to do on their own, had they been in possession of the complete truth of the situation.

Lying or presenting false or misleading information, or withholding vital information, can cause a person to do something they would not have otherwise done. This is the principal aspect of manipulation that is generally undesirable.

This includes: Intentionally pushing emotional buttons to cause the other person to react a certain way. Asking another person to do something, and subtly implying some bad consequence if they do not do it. Presenting a plan to help the other person achieve something purportedly for their benefit, when in fact, it was actually crafted to benefit us. There is an underlying aspect in the last example, and that is hidden or undisclosed intentions. The key is underhanded.

John is committed to a date he made with you earlier in the week. A day later, he met an old flame, Judy. Judy invited John to an event which was to take place on the same date and time as the date with you. John doesn't want to break the date with you, because he had already broken several dates before, giving highly suspect reasons. He tells Judy that he already has tickets to that event, and he will meet with her there because he's working late, and cannot predict the time he'll be available to arrive. He then calls you up and works into the conversation the fact that he heard of an event that he thinks you will like better than the previous plan. On the day of the event, he calls you up, and tells you he's going to work late, and to go ahead, he will meet you there. John goes to the event ahead of you and Judy, and figures out a way of working both of you into a date. Almost a classical situation comedy, and yet, a rather unsavory bit of manipulation. Most of us tend exercise more finesse to put items on a calendar, when we think the other person will surely object if we did so openly. But it is better to discuss and agree on schedules than to manipulate or trick the other person into accepting your preference.

You can do little when you didn't plan the events you wanted to bring about. It is unlikely that you'll be able to see him before he goes out of town on business or a family gathering of some sort when there is little time to plan. It is unreasonable to expect someone to make last minute changes to their plans for you; and if they do, they are likely end up resenting it on some level.

However, communicating is always a profitable activity. Calling him to see if he wants to get together with you before he leaves town can do no harm, providing you give him time to work on it. If he is busy, you won't get him on the phone, so it will be better to leave a message. In fact, since you may run into the problem of finding yourself having to generate spontaneous communication, it will probably work better to leave a message in his answering system, which you have practiced before hand, and might go something like this: "Hi. I've been thinking about you, and thought it would be nice to get together before you leave town. I know you are probably busy, but I thought it would be nice to see you before you leave. If I don't hear from you before you go, I'll give you a call in a week or so. Have a safe trip."

Whether or not this will get him to meet with you before he leaves town, it will at least have a positive effect. You are gently placing yourself in his thoughts. There is no pressure and there are no demands—just a comfortable, warm reach.

If you want him to do something, it is better to persuade him to do so by providing truthful reasoning. Give him all the information you have that could affect his decision. Explain also your own personal feelings and intentions. Divulge even your selfish reasons as to why you would like him to take an action. Finally, give him complete choice over his action or response.

Chapter Seven

Exploring Emotions

Love doesn't make the world go round,
Love is what makes the ride worthwhile.
~ Elizabeth Browning ~

Chapter Eight
Dating Protocols

Protocol is a code of behavior—ways in which people do things in a given culture. How to talk, what signals are appropriate under what circumstances, when to call, and many other rituals of contact. Most books I reviewed on relationships concentrate on protocol. I discuss it in this chapter, but taking up points that I consider important, and adding what has been said by others in order to give you guidelines. This should give you more flexibility in deciding what can be acceptable, or what you can make acceptable by your attitude and approach, than is generally suggested in other texts.

There are as many ways to respond to the actions of others, and as many ways to open up a channel to others, as there are people. If you have questions or thoughts that you feel are not talked about clearly, you are welcome to write me. It is difficult to know whether he has other love interests. Traditionally, men do not make other pursuits and intentions clearly visible to you. At the same time, whether he does have another interest or not, he's at least showing that he's exploring some possibilities with you. If the initial dates didn't add fuel to the fire, what should have happened?

One of the best topics to discuss is the reactions and emotions which brought about the initial attraction. Exploring these things in quiet conversation will stimulate and intensify, once again, the original sensations.

You want to touch upon the same emotional triggers that might have been touched when he first saw you. "What did you see in me that prompted you to approach me?" "Did you feel a funny thing inside you?" "Did you just have sexual reaction or something?" These types of questions will prompt him to open up emotionally. Off the top of his head, he will probably not even know the true answers to these questions. He will have to honestly inspect his feelings or give some superficial answer. Let your intuition guide you in detecting superficial answers, and if that is what you get, simply help him dig a little deeper to find what he is truly trying to say. If he gives answers after some honest consideration, he is giving the connection meaning with his words.

As I said, the truth might not be immediately available to him, so the words he uses to translate the smallest portion of his emotions will construct a slight bond with you in his mind.

There are no restrictions on topics for conversation, provided they are born out of genuine concern for each other. You're your opinions about relationships are a very suitable topic, because they can move the conversation to touch upon the personal practices and beliefs each of you hold. This information will reveal expectations which will affect the relationship you are establishing with him.

Realize that if both of you are too shy to have any meaningful conversation on heartfelt topics and end up discussing nothing more than trivia, you may not be doing what is necessary to fuel the embers of the passion you felt the first instant you met.

If you don't hear from him for a while, you missed opportunities to make a strong contact. Therefore, the connection remains somewhat superficial.

Attitude - Blind Reckoning

At early stages of the connection you have to play it by intuition, which, for all practical purposes means blind reckoning, or navigating by interpretation of signs and instruments, rather than by direct observation.

Attitude is one of the best tools to use when navigating blindly. I will give you some examples and concepts to help you adjust your attitude and approach in this stage of the connection, as a stopgap solution while you learn specific details of navigating with more accurate readings.

The following points are aspects of attitude which you may wish use as guidelines:

* Despite what you may have been led to believe, you, as a woman, have a lot more to offer a man, and a lot more to risk.

* I will continue to insist that you keep your eyes open and don't over focus on a single person at an early stage. Doing so will continuously give you the illusion that you are obligated to make early commitments without having enough certainty. It will also give an illusion of scarcity. Most people handle scarcity by holding on so tight to the other person that it stifles them. There will be those who sweep you off your feet and you will not know what happened. There will be those who touch you with words, and those who, with their actions, show their desire and passion.

* Beware of intentions. Recognize that actions are the result of what is in the mind of a person—a reflection of a person's interests, priorities and intentions. What he does is what he wants to do, even when it is an obligation. When you understand what he wants, you can gauge what you want to do and what you have to overcome if his actions suggest he's not coming close to you. You can then set out to become his priority, if that is your desire; however, at this stage you and your friend are barely at the meeting point in the connection. You have yet to capture enough of his attention to become significantly real in his mind and in his life.

* Avoid the traditional advice of peers who have already misunderstood the basic realities in human interchange. For example, someone will say to you: "You're making it too easy for him. You must call him tomorrow to set some facts straight, rather than continuing these guessing games."

Someone else tells you: "You must demand to know whether he wants to be in touch with you. While you think he's a nice guy and you enjoy spending time with him as a friend, you're getting mixed signals and you don't want that." Yet another suggested you say: "You approach me in the restaurant, take me out, and now want to invite me to your party after not calling me for a month. Then you act as though nothing happened. You just treat me like a good friend, and then disappear." And as if that is not enough, they go on: "I am not necessarily looking for a commitment, but even as friends, I think that I deserve a little more respect. If you can't handle a friendship with me at this point of your life, why don't you just say so, and I will never call you again. We both can go on with our lives as though we never met."

First, remember that you've only had two or three relatively superficial contacts, the restaurant, the party and the rushed phone call. Manners require a bit of moderation with regard to new acquaintances. In this case, setting the facts straight is simply bad form in talking with someone you have just met. It announces a rule of conduct in an area of the relationship that has not yet been developed. You must establish common ground for communication, and `setting the facts straight` is not generally acceptable as an initial approach.

In the next statements, ("... as though nothing happened... I deserve a little more respect...") you are making suppositions that are not real at this stage. He has every right to act as though nothing has happened, because nothing has happened. You are attempting to establish some rules of behavior for a new friend. If he indeed treated you like a good friend, then you're a few points ahead.

Also the statements are contradictory; in one breath you reveal some apprehension as to whether there is a connection or not. In the next breath, you retreat from the non-existent connection: "I'm not looking for a commitment." When a woman says, "let's be friends" he's already wondering why would you want to enforce a friendship if it has not developed naturally? Finally, you are threatening him with returning to a life without you if he doesn't treat you with respect. That is almost humorous.

I give you these examples, because I've heard them enough times in enough variations to know that they are relatively common among many ideologies these days.

* On the opposite side of the fence, you may also be advised by a friend not to call him again: "No, don't call him at all. It's his loss if he does not want to be with you; and if he wants to act indifferent, then let him eat his heart out later on when he wakes up and realizes what he missed out on."

Either approach is a form of manipulation. You are trying to cause him to act in a certain way as a response to your statement.

As I mentioned before, it is very appropriate to communicate something you want to communicate. It is very appropriate to show enthusiasm to reveal your feelings. It is not appropriate at all to manipulate him to make him feel the way you do or behave in the way you want him to. Not now, when you're merely acquaintances, and not later when you become closely connected.

All these are manipulative tactics. In the latter example, you are threatening to punish him if he doesn't behave when he, "wakes up and realizes what he missed out on." You're suggesting he'll experience the suffering from loss that in fact he never had. You will try to make yourself feel comfortable knowing you have punished him for not acting right; the way he should have acted according to your standards. In so advising, your well-intentioned friend is just trying to make you feel better; however, the flavor of the comment may actually embitter you a bit with regard to making connections, something you really don't need.

You have deployed several emotions that will affect what you do and how this whole process comes out. First, you cannot get him out of your mind. This already places you in a position of lesser control. When your mind is gripped by a continuous thought that you cannot remove, then your ability to act is decreased. Second, if after a couple of informal dates where you are not sure what impression you made, you keep looking back to find out what you might have done wrong. This seriously handicaps you because your apprehension will certainly seep through in communications to come. When one person feels apprehension or anguish, the other person senses it and tends to feel pressured. Your apprehension, on the other hand, should be read as a perception that things aren't going quite right. If you have learned to decode your perceptions into real life meanings, you will realize that this is probably correct.

Should I call him? Should I not call him? Should I leave a message? Should I ask him to call me? It is almost impossible to predict a person's thinking or behavior after only a few minor encounters. All that might be applicable is your experience concerning what is traditional—how have others acted in similar situation? Our social standards of behavior change so drastically from group to group, that even traditional behavior will not necessarily provide an accurate guide to what he's thinking about, and why he behaves this way or that way.

When the contact first occurred, there was apparently a strong connection that was probably purely physical. It could have been no more than sensual/sexual vibrations. If that was the case, I would normally predict that he would call back, because each time he remembers that first encounter, he'll feel that same electricity. To say the attraction was physical does not mean that it was not valid.

If a few subsequent encounters do not enhance this electricity, then you have nearly lost the advantage of the irresistible attraction. In this case, to establish a stronger connection you have to exercise other means of developing the connection. This is a good reason to follow your instinct when initiating contacts. Encourage him to go out. Get to know him. Draw him out.

* Don't be afraid to call him whenever you feel like calling him. If he's not there, don't get flustered or worry about how long it takes him to return the call, or if he calls at all. Be genuine. Whatever you say has to be the truth as you feel it. This allows your emotions to flow freely and prevents apprehension At the same time, don't expect him to react in any special way. If you are calling because you simply thought of him, you might say something like, "I called because... suddenly I thought of you, and I just followed the impulse."

* Don't try to do anything to impress him. Just be who you are. After all, if it ever turns into a long-term relationship, you'll eventually want to be able to relax and be yourself! But if you don't start right now, you'll run into problems when you start relaxing later. You will be trapped trying to be someone you are not.

* Earlier, we talked about personal enhancement. The need or desire to change has to be driven by your own personal needs or desires—not necessarily by the wishes of others. Don't change who you are or how you are, unless you want to do so for yourself. Habits and routines are negotiable, but who you are and who you want to be is not necessarily so.

Don't buy into anyone's idea that there is something wrong with you. If you do it will be difficult, if not impossible, to change just to satisfy someone else. If the person you are trying to connect with subtly makes you feel that you are not acceptable, and you begin to believe it, you are in for some rough weather. Start wrapping things up and start looking elsewhere. This applies in all connections.

* Many good people will like you the way you are right now. Many don't know how to show it. Being open and warm toward them will cause them to reveal their true colors. Don't make people earn your affection. If you feel it, give it.

* When it comes to sexual behavior you have to know what you need and want in this area, and work out your own standards. Be conscientious when it comes to things such as health issues and pregnancy. Keep in mind that there are social and economical ramifications if you decide to jump into sex without careful consideration. Don't take risks that will cause your growth and learning from continuing happily. Without going into details, should it ever happen that your connection results in pregnancy, welcome or not, you have the brunt of the work, no matter how good the fellow turns out to be.

If there were one single bit of magic that I could give you that will always work for you, it is this:

* Don't play games with people or think that you can

use strategies to manipulate them. Be the real you that you know yourself to be. Be open and honest, and don't be afraid to get hurt. If somebody disappoints you, don't be too harsh. Let it ride and understand that's part of life. Learn to sense how people are as early as possible in the connection, so you'll know pretty much what to expect, and there won't be any unwanted surprises.

Conversations

* Engaging in small talk is fine, but don't waste too much time with it. Get to the point, and get some agreement on the important things. Leave the light chatter for when you're sitting together giggling about nothing.

Those deadly silences are a frustration no one really wants to experience, so when they happen, put your attention on whether the critical messages have been exchanged or not and bring the conversation in that direction, or simply end it by taking the tension out of the moment, "Jeesh! Looks like we both are at a loss for words. I guess it's a good point to end the conversation, unless you want to say something else." On the other hand, if there is a period of silence and you are comfortable in it, this is probably a good sign. If the connection lasts there will be many comfortable silences to come.

* Making light of embarrassing moments is a worthwhile skill to develop. It takes some practice, but you already know how to do this with people you know well. Use the same techniques with people you don't know as well. They are as human as the ones you already know.

* Calling in person is often more effective if you have a specific and direct message to convey. If the connection seems to be weakening from the original chemistry, personal contact can provide you with opportunities to go beyond the explicit message. Once you have delivered the message which was the purpose of your visit, you can casually go on talking and move on a specific direction. You can simply ask direct questions or make poignant comments, such as, "You seemed very excited about me at the beginning!" These types of questions and comments will draw him out enough for you to understand

what might be going on inside him.

* Avoid questions that might suggest that you're attempting to trap him into making him think he has acted improperly, such as, "You asked me out more at the beginning than now. Are you losing interest?" The line 'are you losing interest' will be usually received as an accusation that he'll have to defend, and most likely he'll feel inclined to skirt the truth. If he had actually considered a reason why he recently began asking you out less, then you can be sure he will not have an answer with which you would necessarily be pleased.

* Trying to corner someone into expressing that he likes you is a subtle form of manipulation. The best way to tell whether or how much he likes you is to read his actions. From his actions we know that he was taken by you at first meeting, so he took you out a couple of times. Then he didn't call for a while and then invited you to a party. This group of actions simply shows that he likes you, but you have not won his heart. He may also be too busy to start an intense relationship. You are being considered, but you're not at the head of his list at this time.

Refining Acquaintances to Meaningful Connections
Now that you have gone through the few initial magical encounters, you are ready to move the connection to a higher level. So far you've just become part of his immediate reality. So you are in! That is to say, you are now a recognizable entity. You are part of his life to some extent.

Now it's a matter of keeping in touch and building it gradually. This involves being attentive to the sensitivities of the other person, some of which has been discussed in the section on manners. Don't attempt to interpret his behavior, or figure out the meaning of actions beyond what is plainly visible. When he says, "Drop in any time," it may simply mean you're welcome, but what is plainly visible is that he assumes you will announce yourself beforehand. Your experience with him can tell you this. Whether you should just stop by unannounced depends on local customs, or on expressed preferences. If you're told, "Drop in tomorrow evening," you are being given the option of an informal visit, and it is up to you to decide whether you're going to simply drop in or call first. It's a judgment call on your part.

* Of course, if you don't feel comfortable going to his house because you suspect he plans to do something inappropriate, then don't go. However, there are just as many opportunities to do the inappropriate elsewhere. Don't try to second-guess him or make calculations on what being invited to his home might mean or not mean. Just trust your inner senses and you'll be fine.

* Traditional behavior should not necessarily be your guide. Keep your eyes open and never doing anything that violates your integrity or your sense of pride and self. But turning down his invitation to his home because of what you have been socially conditioned to believe it might mean is not a good basis for making that decision.

* Give him the benefit of the doubt and be sure you understand what you want. Make certain you maintain your own sense of integrity. You don't have to raise the issue unless something happens that requires it.

* Finally, as you go about developing a connection in earnest, with care and attention, you should also be able to count on a tapestry of meaningful connections which weaves itself almost automatically. This will, no doubt, add to the enrichment of your life, as well as to the lives of those with whom you choose to connect.

The mind set of one's peer circle affects one's ability to establish meaningful connections. One may end up settling for less and making adjustments to fit that mind set, which ultimately will make one's life revolve around someone else's life, upon that person all is dependent, and without whom the world ends. That is a dangerous position to be in.

* At times it is beneficial and soothing to be alone. But that should be a matter of choice, not something that happens because you have too few or no meaningful connections.

* Here is a curious practice that is rarely noticed in the selection of people. We are accustomed to invest incredible

amounts of time and attention on people who don't give us positive attention, and sometimes on those who don't seem to know we exist. Yet many people like us readily, without much effort on our part. Why not extend our sights to notice those who readily like us?

Your first reaction is to say, "Yes, but I don't like him." My answer is, go back to the chapter on self discovery. In reality, there is rarely reason to outright dislike anyone. It's more natural to like than to dislike people, particularly when one has taken the time for self-understanding.

Expanding The Connection Through Sex

So now, lets say you are still together after several dates, and you find yourself a bit more comfortable with one another. You end up hanging out with his friends at his house for a few hours. You may have had a few drinks, and before you know it, it is three in the morning. You are too tired for the trip home. You are invited to stay the night, as you do not want to travel so late.

There are most likely many thoughts swimming around in your head at this point. First of all, let me say that alcohol can take away your inhibitions and make you do things you wouldn't normally do in a more sober state of mind. If you give in to your desires because the alcohol has loosened you up a bit, you may regret your decision. Your inconsistent behavior, whether it is a by-product of alcohol or anything else, can steal a good connection right out from under you.

Let us discuss some of the thoughts that you might be having at this point. Maybe you are thinking that you have to provide sex if you want to keep him. Or maybe you want sex, but don't want to do it so early as to give the impression that you are easy. There is also the nagging thought that he might leave you after he gets what he wants, or the thought that you won't perform to his standards, and will risk losing him to someone more experienced.

Sex is not an act that is separate from the connection you have with this person. It does not stand alone, like a product or a package of something you trade, or use as a gambling chip. Sex is one of the many components of life. While it may need to come into focus at times, it should neither be your primary focus, nor should it be avoided. Your connection is not composed strictly of sex. It is composed of whatever you and the other person decide it shall be composed of. You do not have the duty to provide sex to a man, nor does he have to provide it to you. If you are not completely ready to give yourself to him sexually, make that point clear.

He may want other things, but yes, he wants sex just as much as you do. Earlier I proposed the idea of taking the sex out of the picture to discover what else is involved in the relationship, and whether you or he would even continue the relationship if there were no possibility for sex. Would you continue the connection on the same basis if you knew sex would never be part of it?

Men and women want sex. It is natural to desire sex. Sexual repression in our society is what tends to bring sex to our attention disproportionately. Repression is present when something is heavily regulated, heavily forbidden, heavily shut out of normal conversation. The effect of repression is similar to compressing on a balloon; when you press on one side, the areas not being compressed will bulge out. When frank and open discussions about sex are not available in normal settings, such as home and school, it bulges out through other channels. This creates apprehension, shame, confusion and a host of other emotions which are unclear to the individual for whom these subjects have been declared taboo. Please remember that sex, when treated as a normal part of life, and as a healthy desire, is not only okay, but also very beautiful.

Yes, my dear; he wants sex at some point and so do you. Let nature develop the signs inside you that will tell you when it is right. Don't make outside pressure the principle reason for doing it. If he is intelligent and sensitive, he'll also sense the right time, and there will not be any argument or discussion about when it does or does not happen.

Sexual Practices

Do you remember when the idea of kissing a boy was disgusting?

I want to pass on some important thoughts to make your sexual life pleasant and free from ghosts, shadows, guilt and/or embarrassment. You can also go to a priest, rabbi, pastor, teacher or anyone whose advice you trust. You will get their idea of what is acceptable and what is not. This is fine. However, in order to be certain in your own heart about such things, let me suggest that you seriously consider who might be an authority on the subject. Is any man or woman alive on this planet a more qualified authority on the subject than you? There is no one more qualified to decide what is acceptable or practical for you, than you. This is important, because this is where the struggle sometimes begins. He wants you to do something you don't feel comfortable doing. He tells you everybody does it. You buy into it. Presto! You've just become a slave. Don't do it just because everybody does it! Experiment all you want, but don't allow yourself to be persuaded into doing anything with which you don't feel comfortable. If you are not clear on this, read the section on integrity, and compromise versus agreement.

As for the actual sexual act itself, there are hundreds of well-presented books with pictures on sexual practices as carried out in various societies. If you are a novice or if you don't feel comfortable with the knowledge you have acquired through experience, I advise you to study up a bit, so that the nuances and details are not a mystery to you. From this research, you will be better prepared to form your own ideas and practices.

Ultimately, when looking at sex as an intricate part of a connection, it may first be necessary to get rid of socially acquired misconceptions. What are these misconceptions? To me, a misconception is not based on the act itself, but on the enforced valued placed upon it by others.

You will find males and females who engage in sex for sport. While this may have its attraction to you, as it attracts so many, I would like to point out that it has a limited usefulness. Having sex primarily for physical gratification has become acceptable and will likely continue to be acceptable, even if certain forms of it are made illegal.

When you relate to me the events of a date and make it a point of mentioning that nothing happened, it suggests some imbalance of focus on the sexual relationship. Sex appears to be a main playing piece in today's social game of courtship. You're expected to figure out when it's the exact right time to move the piece. Neither a moment too soon nor a moment later! It appears as if you've been persuaded that sex is the main brick in the foundation of the relationship.

You already made a direct point to him that just because you were spending the night doesn't mean you are ready for sexual contact. You verbally expressed it by announcing that you are only staying provided that sex does not come into play. With that, you're also making an assumption about his intentions in asking you to spend the night. Do you wonder if he would try anything to obtain sexual gratification if you didn't make your intentions clear? Your announcement is posturing. Posturing is presenting a strategy of behavior which, to some degree, may be read as manipulative, rather than a forthright, genuine statement. Maybe the only thing that happened when you spent the night was that you slept in his bed, and all he did was just to hug you all night long. This dance adds to mutual posturing as a prelude to sex.

It is true that sex is a very powerfully connecting event. It seems to open doors which would otherwise never open. Sex is so powerful that it has been known to turn a one-night stand into a lifelong relationship. Be sure you understand what it can do and what you want to do with it.

Chapter Eight — Dating Protocols

The greatest weakness of most humans
Is their hesitancy to tell others,
How much they love them
While they're alive.
~ O.A. Battista ~

Chapter Nine
Reading His Heart

You are frequently concerned about how the man feels about you. Ah! How to tell! If I needed to fill space, I could write a lot about this. But the answer is simple, and it requires very little space.

His intentions are reflected in his actions. People's feelings and intentions are clearly visible in their actions. Actions represent the result of conscious or hidden intentions; accidents are rare.

What he does is what he intended to do. Is he stringing you along? Is he manipulating you? A single action may not serve to tell all; however, over a period of time you will come to realize that his actions are a reflection of his priorities and his intentions.

As you observe a person, even over a short time, you begin to notice style, characteristics, language, and all the elements that eventually form an image of that person in your mind. You can be quite certain that the way the person acts is the direct result of his ideas on how he should be. His actions are a result of his opinions, beliefs, and intentions.

One little flag that should be visible, and an important one, is the fact he talks to you. If he initiates conversations and communicates his thoughts to you, you can be assured that you're on his list. What priority you have on that list varies according to what is going on in his life and how you guide his attention when it comes to relating to you.

Another flag that allows you to understand where you stand is the way he deals with your communication. If you page him or leave a message and he answers instantly, you have become important to him. If he doesn't get back to you for days, it's obvious that, while you may still be on his list, you are not a high priority. There is the possibility that he couldn't call or didn't get your message in time to call fast enough. You will discover soon enough which it is, so try not to become anxious. The fact that he gets back to you at all remains a good sign.

The most difficult flag to interpret is the one which manifests in the total absence of communication. This one usually means that you are no longer on his list.
The best, but not necessarily the easiest thing to do is to cross him off yours. If you still think there are worthwhile qualities which justify pursing the connection, be prepared for some really hard work.
Understanding Motives

The idea of mental connection or spiritual connection with others is gaining greater and greater acceptance, as it tends to explain many different mental phenomena we experience on a daily basis. This is particularly true today with new modes of communication, such as the Internet, where physical contact is less likely. People report finding that they are acquiring certain sensitivities to the understanding of other people they have not and will likely not meet face to face. If you are skeptical or uncomfortable with that concept or with the terminology, think of it as intuition or sixth sense.

For example, you are driving down the street, resolving some problem at work or school, and suddenly you are assailed with an unexpected thought of someone else. It is highly likely that the other person has brought you to their mind at that same moment. But what are they thinking? This alone indicates that you have enough presence in their lives that they feel compelled to think about you. There is an interest as well as a curiosity in their mind about you. It indicates that you've become part of their reality.

The process in the mind or the spirit that we call thinking is not identical from one person to another. Let us say that the process is whatever it is at any given time. It can contain words, concepts, emotions, sensations, and anything you can imagine. Additionally, there are the varieties of conflicts that are relatively natural with most people, and which are part of the contents of their thoughts.

Now let's see how to experience what is likely to be the thought process of others. What do you do to perceive are the contents of that package?

First, understand that it will not always be clear, since thought packages are not always clean in most peoples minds; therefore, you will experience a jumble of thoughts. The easiest process to reasonably understand the contents of a thought package is to simply observe. This means look without attempting to inject logic or rational thinking into the package. In this way you will be able to sense and get a feeling for what is there. You may become apprehensive or experience other discomforts, or simply a feel a peaceful wave. But don't be surprised if what you get is full of confusion.

While your quest is more or less focused on the aspect of an intimate connection, all the components of a human person's life play into this area. Professional decisions, economic decisions, and social decisions—all these things will affect how a person thinks and how they respond to your activity of building an intimate connection with them.

Since apprehension is in some way a state of uncertainty, there is a natural tendency to attempt to resolve it immediately.

This is done much in the same way as I explained in Part Two, Chapter Two, Section "decoding your perceptions." Simply scan the thought package with a broad sweep of your attention. Do not attempt to inject logic or rational thinking into the process. Separate yourself from the situation in order to get a broader view of it. After a while you will hit upon ideas or sensations that appear to resolve the feelings you are exploring. How do you recognize the points of resolution? Normally these points will be accompanied with a relief and a certainty that will come to you from scanning and sweeping the thought package: "Oh! He wants me to call him." Or, "He's having doubts about me." Or, "Somebody is advising him not to bother with me." "I see that he's decided not to call me anymore."

Even if the information is in some way negative to your interests, knowing it will always be accompanied with some relief and an uncanny degree of certainty.

This entire process is not necessarily easy for most people, and it can take years to develop to any degree of accuracy, but it will produce results almost immediately. It is also possible that you will develop your skills in understanding these thought packages rather quickly.

There is nothing terribly mystical about understanding things. Any method of information acquisition is valid, and any information acquired simply adds to the pool of information you normally look at when resolving life problems. You do not have to make a point of telling the other person that you perceived their thought and can read their mind. It is not unusual that all they experience is the confusion of their own thoughts. They won't see your analysis as a valid one. So, while you may consider the information in taking action along a certain path, you needn't debate with the other person about whether or not the information is accurate or not.

Inaccurate Interpretation of Events

Although actions are the result of intentions and desires which reflect a person's priorities, no single action can give you enough of a clue about where another person stands with regard to you. You are advised to base any such judgment on a series of actions.

For example, after the initial contact, you were asked out for two subsequent encounters. This is while the impact of the first strong attraction was still vibrant in the heart and in the mind. Now, the fact that you were asked out doesn't necessarily reveal what kind of connection the other person is seeking to create with you.

Let's say there is no contact for over a month after the

initial dates. Depending on the context, this should not be interpreted strictly as a negative sign. During holidays, for example, people will have had plans with others for some time. You cannot expect someone to change his schedule to accommodate you, a new connection. Also, he may have other commitments to someone who might have been in his life before you came along. That he approached you doesn't mean he was alone. Remember, that initial fire is something quite difficult to set aside, so he took action by approaching you while your interest was high in order not to risk a cool down on your part. However, he does most likely have other obligations, which cannot be set aside.

As I said, just because the guy asked you out doesn't mean he needed or was looking for a romantic connection. Maybe he simply reacted to the overwhelming electricity. To assume there are rational intentions behind his reaching toward you may be an incorrect assumption. You will try to explain it to yourself and he might try to explain it to you. But what you are basically observing in yourself and the other person is a reaction to the magnetic connection.

That behavior is then tempered by other events in his life. For example, one explanation to his style of behavior can quite easily be traced to his profession. Demands are placed on him to maintain certain contacts and attend certain events and activities related to his profession.

Now, as I had predicted, he calls you and invites you out again. It would be easy to predict his calling. Remember the initial fire you felt, and notice how you are still cooking inside! This immediately shows the extent to which he was exposed to the same fire. The fire is difficult to ignore for long, and he would feel compelled to call to see what might develop. Now, however, he's being a bit more cautious, since during the first two dates nothing happened to turn the spark into a blazing fire. Polite, superficial conversation is not what you might consider good fuel for the embers of the heart.

There seems to be a generally accepted notion about what a man wants from a woman. I've come to boil it down to two basic possibilities: One, he's interested in obtaining sexual gratification; two, he has serious intentions.

Serious intentions do include sexual gratification as one of the components. To assume otherwise is courting disappointment and shock. That's not to say that sexual gratification is the principal objective, but, quite frankly, it is an important one. Understanding that the magnetic connection occurred predominantly on a physical plane (albeit there has to have existed an additional connection on a mental and spiritual level as well) it remains clear that sexual attraction is an important driving force. The sexual energy and the sensual energy amongst humans is beautiful in itself, and it is one of the most powerful energies humans are capable of experiencing.

The fact that he made no advances along this line can be an indication that he's shy, or he is convinced it is inappropriate at this point. He may have sensed you were not ready to accept. So he didn't want to ask risk the embarrassment of being turned down.

Well, you tell me this is not the real objective—that you connect on many other levels, and you feel this wonderful thing and that wonderful thing, and it's not just sex. I agree, it's not just sex; but sex is indeed a necessary and most important component at this stage, even when neither of you would admit so. Consider the following: are you prepared to pursue the connection with the understanding that sex will never be part of it?

You would most likely abandon the connection if there were no possibility of sexual gratification. Would you abandon the relationship if intellectual or spiritual connections were absent, as long as the sexual potential was present?

Don't Want You Getting Hurt

After you have been dating for a while, you have become a vivid part of his reality. When you see each other he tends to act as though you are his girlfriend. He is very gentle-mannered, sweet and respectful, and you feel very comfortable, as if you've known him for a long time. This might puzzle you if in an earlier date he said, when discussing his relationship with you, that he didn't want you to get hurt.

What is he talking about? What potential hurt could there be from any relationship? Well, when a connection breaks up there is a great deal of hurt that accompanies the break up. What is behind that statement is, "The way I feel about you, or the way I am, makes it a high probability that we will not last."

The process that brings this about is somewhat complex. It has to do with the wide variety of social differences in courting practices and the changing attitudes in such practices, as well as economic considerations and long-term survival safeguards that people feel they need to take into account.

Thinking back to your teens, you may remember a fairly rigid system for making connections. People usually paired off very soon after discovering a mutual attraction. During that period of time, this pairing off was considered somewhat sacred in its exclusivity. Talking with any real interest with someone else, even on a friendly basis, was usually considered a betrayal of sorts. This method of courting remains relatively predominant in many social settings, and many people in the American culture have a tendency to maintain this narrow perspective, which continues well into middle age and sometimes into the autumn and winter of life.

At the same time many people, male and female, understanding the futility of such methods, strive for freer practices. They do not wish to maintain an exclusive dating relationship, because they understand they want to remain continuously open to the option for other types of connections. There is also the possibility that they themselves know they are not going to make any promises that will end up hurting them as well. In other words, they are avoiding setting themselves up to get hurt while at the same time leaving new avenues open.

So it is possible that when a man tells you he doesn't want to hurt you, he perceives you as someone who regards exclusive dating as the proper method of sustaining a connection, and fancies himself as a non-follower of such traditions. He knows that he is not ruling out the possibility of finding or creating other connections. He is acting out a personal belief or personal policy. He is aware that violating what he thinks is your standard will cause a rift in the connection and, therefore, the potential hurt. He also knows that if he does date others you might be hurt, and he has a sense that it will happen.

Many social changes are taking place in the way we connect. The young observe that their parents have gone their separate ways. Connections are of an entirely different nature than adolescents had been led to believe, such as the mating for life ideal. Relationships with schoolmates one knew in early years, is rare.

We also see more and more the vitality of connections being dependent on economic conditions, and very careful planning into the future. Connections begin to revolve around our professional lives, which has become a major, if not the only social life we have.

The uncertainty of a professional future seems to guide many into a non-committal arrangement with connections, leaving themselves open and available for opportunistic connections which might become additional security to their future. This is true to a meaningful extent, and it is so not only with women, but with men as well.

So at any time that there are such major social shifts, the conflict between the traditional and the newer trends becomes difficult to ignore. The traditional standards begin to break down and gradually give way to new trends. There is no clearly visible trend that one might either observe, much less, be required to follow.

Yet, on some level, it's possible to transcend traditions or modern tendencies, in relationships where you might strike one another's mind and emotions so deeply that you become enraptured, and willing to change generally accepted practices.

If a current connection doesn't work out, don't fret. If you see it objectively, nothing is lost. View endings as opportunities for new beginnings. You always gain another perspective and more knowledge about what you seek. No connection is ever really lost unless it is neglected or ignored. So long as there is some genuine communication, there is always the opportunity to develop a meaningful connection.

Habits

There are many characteristics which people display on a continual basis. It is important you understand this because you need a way of predicting what things will be like in times to come. There is a popular refrain I heard a few years ago which quite appropriately illustrates what you might find in any connection. The refrain says: "The first time, it was an honest mistake; the second time, a careless indiscretion; the third time, a habit." This means that when you see repetitive action you can be certain that you will continue to see it on a relatively permanent basis. Changing habits is a major undertaking for any human, and usually attempts to change another or one's own habits are accompanied by severe mood and character shifts. If a change does take place, one tends to feel that one is not oneself.

Often these types of experiences, observations, and accompanying insights are apparent to people who are faced with partners who have extreme behavior patterns, such as abuse, alcoholism or other forms of socially stigmatized behavior. Yet, it is applicable to the entirety of daily activities and behavior. Thus when you've recognized a habit in your potential mate that you find unacceptable, you have several alternatives, and they do not involve changing the other person.

The first response is simply a choice that you will not live with it under any circumstance. The second is the choice to endure it.

The third is to overcome that weakness within you that causes you to be wounded by it. This is the most difficult solution to implement, because it's difficult to see that what we abhor in others are unseen aspects of ourselves. Also we often base our decisions to change ourselves motivated by social acceptability. When the flaw we see in another is socially unacceptable, we are less likely to come around to accepting it. For example, everybody knows it's unacceptable to lick your fingers while eating. Instead of bothering to change our attitude, and becoming more accepting and tolerant, we demand that the other person change or eliminate the habit or addiction. Conversely, if it is our habit that annoys the other person, especially if such a habit is socially acceptable or condoned, we are less inclined to make changes in ourselves.

The choices above should be made early in the development of the relationship; before any major commitments are made. Once commitments have been made, the only real viable solution is to change our own ability to accept and embrace the other person's habits, whether socially acceptable or not.

Intuition Versus Extra-Sensory Perceptions

We are exploring ways of increasing our wisdom through understanding, and the expansion of perceptions in order to achieve that understanding. The area of extrasensory perception and psychic viewing are possible ways of gaining understanding. Extra-sensory perceptions and psychic abilities refer to the perception of things by means beyond the physical senses.

Some degree of validity can be contemplated with regard to our sixth sense, due to the perception of plausible evidence. However, after extensive study of this area, I have observed that these perceptions are not predictably reliable. One reason is that there is sufficient information to suggest that such perceptions are not purely in the physical dimension. Therefore, the time frames within which things are perceived are rarely related to a discernable real world time frame, making a reliable connection to real world events, difficult.

Psychic perceptions may be no more than mental projections of current physical perceptions that are a natural function of intellect to predict the future. It is my tendency to assume that this might be an intellectual and an intuitive capacity that can be developed to a great degree of accuracy. Some of the attributes of psychic perceptions are the same as those attributed to intuition. Intuition is also generally understood as a sense acquired from the accumulation of experiences and extrapolations thereof.

There are some things I think you can do and may find workable. When you have perceptions of things you believe to be beyond the physical, explore them to see how they eventually translate into the physical realm. Once you are able to establish some patterns, then you will be able to understand what certain perceptions are connected to, as discussed in the section "Decoding your Perceptions and Emotions." The same drills discussed there can be done to decode any type of perception.

Thus Far, Well Enough?

Now you have been seeing him for several months. If you managed to do at least some of the things we talked about, you will begin to have a good sense of where things are.
Let's say things are going along pretty well, but his actions don't give you a clear idea of his intentions. Maybe he forgets to call you when he is busy. Or maybe he lets so much time pass between calls that you become unsure again and start questioning the relationship

Earlier I pointed out that when a pattern begins to appear, realize it is a pattern. Remember that habits are exposed by their repetitiveness. If this random style of getting in touch with you is habitual, it's up to you to decide whether you can live with it.

You have the option of structuring your contacts to make it easier by simply ending your conversations with more definite statements about your next contact.

Is he really that busy? Is his professional career so pressured that it creates some unpredictable events in your life. Is he playing hard to get? What is there to "get" that you don't already have? I assure you, unless you have grossly misjudged his character, he's not calculating or scheming to make things difficult for you. He is simply going about his life, enjoying his connection with you. Your objective to establish an easy-going, free-flowing connection has been achieved. Now, if you simply follow the points outlined in the section on communication, you should have no problem maintaining the connection at a level that meets your needs.

If you think something is missing, you should try to define more clearly for yourself what it is that you expect. If you have met your objectives, the task now is to simply maintain clear communication and enjoy what you and he have created.

Chapter Nine   Readng His Heart

When fairy tales and fantasies happy ending has come to life in the form of a potentially meaningful connection, you realize that it is only the beginning, and that you will have to create the realities you dreamed about. There are things you can do to develop and grow stronger and happier. They are not necessarily born in you. You must work at it. This is the dawning phase; you awaken, and begin to construct the building blocks to strengthen the connection.

Part III
The Dawning

We are all born for love...
it is the principle existence and it's only end.
~ Disraeli ~

Chapter Ten
Communication

What people understand, sense, and perceive are the realities by which they run their lives. The most important tool we use to examine and exchange understanding about realities is communication, and I would be neglecting this most important tool if I didn't at least discuss the basic ideas.

Communication between people consists of transferring an idea or reality from one person to the other. The communication can be understood to be complete if the receiver has a clear duplicate of what the sender intended. I emphasize duplicate because we often think that an approximation is enough. It might be at times, but it should not be a routine style of communicating. Doing so will simply pile up confusion between those involved in the communication.

One can consider the method of transmission, whether in words, gestures, writing or thought, as part of the communication. The critical element however is the event of an exact duplicate at the receiving end as was delivered at the source. Other elements, often overlooked, are the roles played by attention and intention. We often hear people blaming the listener for failure to understand. "You don't understand me." "You misunderstood me."

The person with the idea has the advantage since he likely has the greatest understanding of what he wants to communicate, and therefore has the greater responsibility as to ensure his listener understands. If the intended receiver of the communication has not acquired an exact copy from the sender, then it is the sender's failure.

In simple terms: if you want someone to understand something about you, it's up to you to see that that he or she does. In the early stages of the connection this becomes the most important element. How do I talk to him? What do I say? Give clear messages. The message has to have the information you want him to understand. Consider also the response you expect as a result of the information you provide. What works best is to simply tell him exactly what it is you want him to understand, and what you want him to do.

"I'm going to out of town for a few days. I was hoping we could get together before I left. I realize that this is a busy season, and you might already have plans. I'm letting you know in case you have some time free. Please call me Monday afternoon and let me know whether you can make it."

Straight forward—nothing more than the information you want to communicate. Make it direct and sincere by the intonation of voice. Difficulties and misunderstandings can be avoided early on with clean, clear ways of communicating. Learning how to communicate also involves use of language. The content of what you are communicating must be easily understood. You must employ a relatively organized method of exchanging information, feelings and creative ideas. Additionally there is the instrument which will carry the communication. This is the medium with which you use to transfer your thoughts. Let's look at various components of communication.

Mechanics

These are the basics, which you should understand and develop into habits.

A mechanical explanation of effective communication is, essentially, the process where one person (the sender) transfers an idea into the mind of another (the receiver). The objective is that the receiver gets the same idea as the sender. This requires, more than anything else, the mental desire to get the idea across as precisely and accurately as possible, focusing attention to ensure the sender is aware of what is taking place at the receiving end.

With the same mental attitude, the receiver has the responsibility to achieve an understanding. This is not necessarily a mere recognition of words and their meanings. Understanding requires at least the temporary assumption of the sender's viewpoint in order to process the information correctly.

To illustrate this with a very simple example, let's take a child who has just been given a plate of spinach. He tells his mother, "I don't like this. I don't want to eat it." How do you deal with this? The first action is to simply listen and know what the child has said. Secondly, you must understand how this information is true and valid for the child. This requires taking the child's viewpoint; feeling from inside the child's mind and heart, sensing the emotions of the child, tasting what the child tastes, even when the child has not yet taken a bite of the food. What perception has the child encountered which he finds objectionable? Ultimately, if you cannot achieve the conviction that, from the child's viewpoint, he is right, you can be sure that you have not achieved the understanding required to deal successfully with the information.
Apply this style of listening and understanding in your adult communications, and you will generally have success in the activity of exchanging ideas.

Content

The ideas that you transfer to others, by whatever means, contain information about your perception of reality, and other things which are connected to that reality, such as hopes, dreams and fantasies. When I speak of reality, I'm simply referring to what the individual perceives, through any method of reception, and that which he or she now considers real. The ideas that you transfer to others, by whatever means, contain information about your perception of reality and other things which are connected to that reality, such as hopes, dreams and fantasies. Quite often we experience other people's realities to be quite different from our own. We are often quick to disagree and we promptly dismiss others' realities as strange, to say the least. By the same token, we can assume that they often dismiss our realities as readily as we dismiss theirs.

In establishing good communication, we have the responsibility of presenting our reality with the intention of making it acceptable to others. We must also take the additional responsibility of accepting others' realities as valid. Practicing and understanding the mechanics explained above is essential for turning what may first appear as adverse realities into common realities. Common realities are the glue which bonds and strengthens our connections.

Medium

Often the medium has given meaning to a method of communication in addition to the explicit content of the message. There are differences between leaving a phone message, writing a letter or an email, sending a picture, and talking face to face with someone. Often the meaning is implied, like sending flowers, or giving a holiday gift. As you can see, the medium, that is, the substance or channel that carry the communication (flowers, letter), may affect the meaning of the intended communication. In order to determine which might be the best medium to use at any given time, there are several simple questions you can ask which will usually give you an adequate solution:

Which would be the simplest way of saying it clearly and effectively? What method do most people use to say this sort of thing? How would I feel if I received that communication by the same method? While not everyone would feel the same when contemplating such questions, it is a fair guideline because there are enough similarities amongst individuals in a given social setting that responses would not be too widely diverse.

Manners

I include manners in the communication section because

Chapter Ten — Communication

it is the first mode of communication. Before any exchange of ideas can begin, there is the visual and mental connection that establishes the understanding of what form the communication that follows will take. We are essentially saying that we can and will follow established agreements on how to communicate.

Let's begin the most important and somewhat universal element of protocol (manners) with which you should guide your actions as much as possible:

* Do whatever you promised you were going to do.

Sometimes you make impossible promises, and even if the other person understands they were impossible, you'll find yourself embarrassed to explain why you could not do what you said you would. All this plays along with the idea of considering the other person's importance. It is a good idea not to make firm time promises or commitments unless there is a real need for it, like meeting for a time-sensitive event. If it should be the case that you later discover you made a mistake, notify the other person as soon as possible that you're not going to be able to do something you promised.

* We usually hear the word respect tossed around with the presumption that everybody knows what it means, and surely how it translates into action. Respect: If you were making up new words using existing words, which simply expressed common actions, you might do what the ancients did, for example, in Latin. They took two words: re = again, and specere = to look, to view, to contemplate. Imagine what they might have meant when they created this word. We can say that the extended or additional attention we gave another person, by looking again was called respect. The person had something about him or her that caught one's attention, something attractive perhaps, or something of importance. Any dictionary will give you something approximate to this: To take notice of; to regard with special attention; to regard as worthy of special consideration, to heed.

How can we translate into a style of behavior? Act as though the person you are talking to is the most important person in the world to you. Saying, act as though means to feel the other person's importance. Don't pretend it.

If you mentally and visually look at a person and contemplate their image and presence with a desire to fully understand who they are, you will begin to sense their innate importance. It is not a process of elevating another above oneself or diminishing one's own importance; it is recognizing the presence and importance of the other individual. The more you do this, the more people will like you, because you are showing by your actions that you appreciate who they are. Your actions are saying that you consider people important. Any less than that is tantamount to breaches of etiquette.

* The word respect implies attention, and importance. These three words embody all rules of etiquette ever written, and their application will generally be found in compliance with rules of etiquette, regardless of culture.

Written Communication

When you put something in writing it is there to be seen and read again and again. There are definitely good reasons for not neglecting this method of communication. It gives the writer an opportunity to consider his ideas, and craft them carefully to ensure accuracy. Often a message does not get across to another because of its complexity. Putting things in writing gives the recipient the opportunity to examine the ideas with more care and more attention. Furthermore, the recipient is not obligated or pressured into stopping something else to listen to you. He is able to give full attention to your words on his own time. Sometimes your ideas are so extensive that they loose value or impact if simply spoken. Take the time to write them down.

Written communication generally has a more profound effect on the reader. Three or four paragraphs in a note expressing even mild affection can produce a more powerful effect than if they had been spoken. So when you have something important to say, that is to say, you want your communication to be given special attention, then, by all means do it in writing.

Communication Creates Reality

At the beginning we spoke of the connectivity of life. I think it is important to emphasize connectivity. There is nothing in existence that is totally isolated and independent. When you consider your own personal advancement, consider it with the knowledge and resolution that any understanding contributes to the greater understanding of life and self. All learning will sooner or later connect up with prior learning. The natural process of the mind and its curiosity is to connect new observations to prior experiences and lessons in life. If you have been trained to curb this natural tendency, you should re-establish it as a habitual approach to life.

Your success with connections will be thoroughly related to things not only discussed in this manual, but to everything with which you come into contact. There are more vivid examples of the interconnectedness of things in life in relationships and connections. The general success with connections seems to forecast the success you will have in other areas of life.

You are now aware of the many components of communication, including language and media. Broad exposure to the communications of others, written, visual or verbal, is essential to the development of your own communication skills. Your own expressions of your ideas through writing and oral means should not be ignored. At the very least, you should maintain a notebook wherein you can write your thoughts and experiences which are worthy of note.

To ensure your emotional and social success in the management of connections and relationships, it becomes necessary to make the connection active, so that it will contribute to the mutual enhancement of the parties involved.

There are the general areas to which relatively precise actions can be applied. I use the term engage to help visualize a linking of gears in order to achieve motion. This is creativity through the exchange of ideas and the building of common realities. Common realities are some of the strongest adhesives that bond people.

We often say, when unable to reconcile differences of opinion, "Let's agree to disagree." However, this stance invariably creates or allows the existence of a wall to exist. It clearly delineates boundaries. If we count on one another to take certain actions in situations that require action when the underlying opinions vary significantly, the actions we take will conflict. Different realities are the opposite of common realities. It may be easily acceptable to have philosophical differences so long as no action is required; but when action is required, a coincidence or similarity of reality is necessary. Without a common ground, conflict is inevitable and separation is unavoidable.

A very important action to engage others, is the genuine expression of your feelings about the other person; your expression of liking them, your honest expression of admiration for a particular quality about them that truly touches you. Your actions may clearly show others that you like them. Telling them that you do gives them verbal confirmation that reinforces the perceived reality. Such reinforcement always brings people a little closer.

Chapter Ten

Communication

Love is the master key that opens the
gates of happiness.
~ Oliver Wendell Holmes ~

Chapter Eleven
What is Love

Who does not seek love, whatever that may be!

There are significant variations in understanding the word love, what it means, what it is, what must be understood about it and why such things must be understood.

This broad confusion on the subject is not for lack of intellectual capacity on the part of the population, but the result of a mixture of authoritative discourse in conflict. All these ideologies filter into the social fabric with significant distortions. Added to that are people's own individual perceptions of the abstract nature of love.

Sometimes, classifying love into types can be helpful, but I think it is generally meaningless for the purpose of understanding it. Classifying love in such a way is frequently a method to regulate behavior or excuse it. Each type becomes associated with certain behavior. I don't think that leads to understanding or creating love.

I have intentionally avoided the standard discussions on the subject because it is not my intention to clarify ideas others have presented. I prefer to launch right into what I think is a fresh view on the subject of Love.

When we say a person is beaming, we are suggesting there is a pleasant emanation from them. When we are in the presence of someone who is annoyed, angry or sad, we again experience an emanation from that person which announces to some degree the nature of the feeling they are experiencing. These emanations vary in intensity and are most definitely perceptible by most people.

It is useful to refer to these emanations as energy because we conceive it to have similar characteristics to our scientific concept of energy. It is a physically palpable thing; it can be felt in the body. It may be understood as a form of vibration, a beat that pulsates many times per second.

A metaphor is a type of expression in words which uses a physical event to explain an abstract idea. For example, we say, "When it rains, it pours." That is a metaphor using rain to explain a more abstract idea: abundance, when something arrives, it arrives in large quantities.

To create our own metaphor, let us say that love is something that happens when two energies vibrate in resonance. For instance, to expand on an earlier idea, when combining notes of an instrument, some notes sound good together and others may not. When they work well together there is a harmonic resonance being created by the two notes.

Harmonic resonance is energy resulting from combination of two or more energies. The combining energies have a beat which seems to match in some way harmoniously.

The event of striking a harmony creates a third sound. Love!

Many adults, who have been hearing music indiscriminately may not notice a third sound (and perhaps more!) arising from the playing of two notes simultaneously; however, I've tested children and have found they usually hear more than two sounds when two musical notes are struck simultaneously, for example, on a piano.

This analogy is given to help present an image of harmonic resonance. I do not want to imply that there is an accurate scientific parallel. I am using it metaphorically.

When people understand each other, there is a harmonic resonance. People having things in common will enjoy some level of harmony. People sharing a sexual attraction will enjoy very intense harmonic resonance. People who are of similar emotional disposition tend to achieve a level of harmony. People whose speed of exchange of ideas is synchronized will enjoy a degree of harmonic resonance: There you are sitting, minding your own business, and in an enchanted moment you look across the room, and there he is, looking at you and you feel something new inside you. Harmonic resonance!

Beyond the metaphor I'd thought I might also simplify the concept of love as a deep awareness of connection. This assumes a connection that brings beings together in some form of likeness. This often very deep affinity is sufficiently broad to encompass such things as cannot be explained otherwise. Without a clear understanding of this affinity or awareness of connection, we cannot use it to build love. This awareness or affinity may seem unrelated to harmonics. Whatever the metaphor you choose, this awareness of connection appears to have an element of harmonic magnetism which produces the various sensations and feelings in the body with which we're familiar. It is not uncommon at first to think this type of energy is independent of sexual attraction; however, there is a great deal of sexuality in it, though at this stage it appears to be on a different dimension. That's it! Love!

The good news is that you both felt it. Even better, you have the ability to make this happen with many people. You will understand why this is good news when you are faced with the waning of this feeling later in your relationship, something we will cover later in this book.

Unreality, Disagreements, Differences & Choices

Reality and love are directly proportional to each other. To the degree that unreality (that is, religious, political, and other personal disagreements) is injected into the connection, i.e.: relationship, love will decrease. A change in one will affect the other and vice versa. Consider what happens when you tell someone about something that is close to your heart, something about which you have a strong interest. The other person immediately brightens up and says, "Oh! I like that. It is my favorite hobby. I have a room full of stuff like that."

You have thousands of little examples of times when you liked someone a little bit more, simply because they had something in common with you or understood and agreed with some idea of yours.

Beyond the many variable personal realities, there are the not so common realities of daily existence, religion, politics and social mores with which we are faced. These realities are the essence of personal integrity: a sense of consistent truth underlying one's behavior and personal objectives. Integrity is one of the underlying reasons for actions one takes. Differences or similarities in these realities affect the selection of associations or connections.

If differences exist which do not disturb or do not cause the objectives of the individual to swerve, then it is fair to assume that the differences are safe to the connection. For example, an individual's profession can force one person into a radically different lifestyle from the other. Different religious beliefs can cause similar radical changes. You have to ask, "Is this safe for the connection? Is it acceptable?"

However, if your personal desires call for a high level of closeness, you should understand that such closeness depends a great deal on ever-increasing shared realities.
Seeing things eye-to-eye with another is an important element in any connection. This means some degree of coincidence of reality—some level of agreement on philosophies of life, behavior, experiences, and other areas of importance. Relationships are created or dissolved by the harmony or discordance of reality. Therefore it is important to have some sense of how reality is acquired, built and changed.

Earlier we discussed the idea of repeated exposure as a means of becoming familiar to others so they will find it easier to approach you and talk to you. Repeated exposures are the essential ingredient to the creation of reality.

Consider the method by which an infant acquires a reality of his environment. His method is by repeated observation until objects in his environment accumulate in layers of images which, over time, acquire a degree of solidity which then become the infant's reality. There is no logic, no intellectual information discussed. It is simply repeated exposure. This is also true with adults. It might be called conditioned reality; a reality which has been assimilated through no other means than repetition.

The concept is utilized quite effectively in the advertising and marketing world. If you wish someone to acquire an interest in what you have until they will eventually want it for themselves, you have to mold their reality until the idea of acquiring it seems quite natural.

Instruction, training and education quite often move in the direction of repetition of ideas and concepts with the purpose of making them a part of the trainee's reality in order to provide the tools necessary to complete tasks.

Be aware of how repeated exposures affect your reality and their reality in the pursuit of a connection.

The initial fire may have caused you to overlook the absence of common realities in areas of importance. You've acknowledged that there is that special something, that zing of desire and fire, that burning passion—the feeling that your life would be nothing without him. You are about to embark on the process of evaluating and learning how to move forward with this new connection.

If you didn't have the opportunity of applying evaluation techniques presented earlier in the book, you may find yourself working the evaluation process from the back end. We often allow the zing to take us over before we know that the person is a good potential connection on other important levels, unleashing our passion, throwing caution to the wind.

Maybe we simply couldn't help it!

When the fire is strong, and some of the more important realities are in unison, the idea that "love resolves everything" becomes the rule. We say, "We will be able to resolve anything that comes up." This is possible with the earnest application of conflict resolution discussed later.

If conflicts appear insoluble, the first step, of course, is to go back to the section on meeting people and start the process over. If you are locking horns on small things, you'll burn up into a pile of dust in short order. You need to be prepared for your next encounter; start looking from scratch.

If now you have a connection that is fairly strong, it is time to learn about each other on a deeper level.

There are two methods of approach that come to mind: one is the careful approach, where you gradually fish for common realities. The other is the daring approach, where you simply allow a mind dump from both sides and let the chips fall where they may. What I mean by mind dump is just telling all, and asking the other person to do the same.

Agreement Versus Compromise

Shared and common realities are important ingredients in connections. They most definitely are important if the connection is to achieve a stronger, long-lasting bond. If that is your objective, then you must take into consideration methods of achieving these common and shared realities already discussed.

To convert disagreement into common reality without compromising your integrity, here are some guidelines that will help:

Important truths and realities are created by agreement. Differences are reconciled by agreement. Agreement suggests a rational review resulting in new understanding of new truths being recognized and accepted by all parties.
Procedural truths (how to do things) or realities can be reconciled or created by compromise. Compromise suggests the acceptance of an outcome not entirely of one's preference, but not entirely unacceptable.

By examination you determine what is important or trivial through the examination of your values. A general guideline to make a determination is this: What are the consequences of a new agreement or compromise? Am I extending toward a wider and wider sphere of influence as an individual?

Example (intentionally extreme for illustration): You do not believe in physical punishment as a workable way of raising children. What is the degree of importance of this point? The idea may have visible effects on you as a person. The belief may extend its influence, affecting others around you. Your opinions or feelings may affect the way neighbors behave toward their children, or how a local school sets its policy.

That concept may be an important truth within your reality. According to the statement concerning important truths it would be a violation of your personal integrity if you were to change your position without having arrived at the change through an honest assessment, achieved through real and deep understanding of all aspects of the change.

Here is an example of a trivial or procedural truth: Let's say you don't care for a certain type of music. A change by compromise would entail your having to listen to such music from time to time, even if you don't like it. It is doubtful that such compromise would damage your integrity in any way. You might even grow to like it if you are willing to open your mind to it.

Serious differences will create walls beyond which neither will go. Let's suppose your beliefs require that he must somehow change something about himself, such as his religion or other strong beliefs or ideas, and you find him quite willing to make the change. Why would he make such change? Here are some possible reasons:

The person has no rigid realities about one idea or another, nor will ever have the same fervor toward the idea being embracing. It is a strategic action to retain a vested interest in the connection. The bond will not be viable in the present of many such changes.

The person may as well lack integrity in that area. If the person is willing to change easily and quickly upon your request, without truly understanding the change, and has not arrived at the change as a result of some earnest reevaluation, recognize that such volatility could signal a potential lack of integrity. It also signals a potential lack of predictable stability or predictable evolution to truly suit your purposes. It is also possible that those issues are not a matter of integrity to the other person. If they are for you, then, his easy acceptance may not necessarily be a good connecting element.

Integrity and Truth & Trust

Integrity is the state in which a relative absence of internal conflict is enjoyed, and where a high level of certainty of one's truths, and the resolve to act on them exists. When you act on these truths you will begin to live with a sense of honesty which in turn provides you with a clean conscience concerning your actions.

There is a caution here. If you fixate on one particular truth your life will not change thereafter. If you live only by a limited number of truths, your life will reflect only those truths in its evolution. This may or may not be acceptable to you. But keep in mind that it will prevent you from evolving. Truths change with new observations and new understandings. The truths of youth tend to give way to deeper truths of life experiences and explorations of self. When you allow yourself the freedom to observe new truths, you are more likely to move through life with greater understanding with each passing day.

It is difficult to determine what is true, what is missing and what is false in an environment where most people's reality is manipulated by controlled information.

Let us concern ourselves with truth in relationships. For our purpose, when I talk about truth, I mean accurate information concerning facts, events, perceptions, ideas, thoughts, and any relevant details, and information that would vitally affect the connection or relationship.

When considering the formation of intimate and meaningful connections, one must be totally open and up front on all levels. Any other approach will ultimately backfire.

What about trust? How can I trust everyone I meet so immediately? This is a good point. We have discussed methods of improving perceptions so as to be aware with whom we are making contact. It is vital that you expand and improve your ability to know whom you are coming in contact with.

Beyond that, and in short order, I have found through practice and observation that being fearlessly open has a far greater benefit overall than it has potential harm. I have often advised: Trust implicitly, unless and until given reason to do otherwise.

The results of this attitude are quite interesting. When you trust and are open immediately, any potential betrayal of that trust will surface and become visible within days of the contact. On the whole, people have nothing to protect at an early stage of a contact. Therefore, if someone is habitually untrustworthy, the habit will betray him immediately. This means that you will be betrayed; but it will be in relatively small, inconsequential matters, before the connection progresses deep enough to where a betrayal could be of greater harm.

Untrustworthy people are a minority. It is good to come to know and understand, and be able to discover who these people are, so you can act accordingly.

Let me emphasize that I mean this approach to apply when contemplating meaningful connections, and not necessarily always in all social context. In a Public Relations world where image is important, it is likely that most people tend to be selective concerning what they present to others in terms of information and images of who they are. There are social trends that suggest what to say to whom, and when. The phrase "Familiarity breeds contempt," is a direct expression concerning the socially acceptable behavior of not becoming too familiar, not daring to reveal the inner self.

It is, therefore, not unlikely that you may already find yourself in a relationship where you have entered through the PR doors, gradually building acceptable realities about yourself. This may be suitable early in the connection: It gives you the same leeway of gradual exposure through acceptable manners, and methods of communication. However, this may have landed you in a situation where you are holding back certain things that will eventually necessarily change the image you created at first contact. In this case, consider that the longer you hold back, the greater the potential blow up of such façade.

Information will have to surface at some point; any information withheld presents a barrier to the achievement of any meaningful closeness. The revelation of the information at a point too late in the development of the connection may blow up the connection. If you are afraid to blow it now, by early revelation, what makes you think it would be less severe later? To prevent huge blow up, you have to go back and propose new agreements based on a new foundation. This approach may prevent or salvage a blow-up.

Do I tell if I have Cheated?

If you wonder whether you should tell, realize that the connection was already at risk since it appears to have been subject to unspoken conditions that were brought into the connection at the beginning. The problem here lies in the fact that anything withheld will remain as a barrier to closeness. If this is not intolerable, you might find yourself with no other choice than to keep things where they are; though this is ill advised.

If you are seeking a stronger, closer connection, you will have to go to square one, as suggested earlier. Approach the current connection as if it were a brand new connection and start building things from scratch, and hope that at some point you will be able to clear up these barriers. When the information withheld is particularly unacceptable, such as cheating, hidden motives or ulterior motives, you have to set the stage for openness by building new realities together about forgiveness, acceptability, and conflict resolution. Upon that stage revelations become attainable.

Obviously you are operating with the notion that your

information is unforgivable. Therefore, you find yourself attempting to change the mood into one of forgiveness, for you know otherwise you will suffer the consequences. It is a trap with many trap doors. I'm showing you a way out of the labyrinth because your fears don't allow you a more direct way. I would personally take the direct route of immediate confession, and take whatever the consequences. If I fancy myself as a forgiving person, wouldn't it be better to stay connected to someone just as forgiving? If they choose not to forgive, and break off the connection, what have I lost?

If the connection is already in a process of dissolution, and parties feel that no further efforts in repairing it are worthwhile, there is really no reason to wound one another by revealing a string of acts of deceit. Nevertheless, becoming open at this point has been known to repair dying connections. It is extremely risky if not supervised tightly by a professional, and even then, the results can be doubtful. Both parties involved must have a strong desire for reconciliation.

The best policy is to start out open and forgiving and allow growth, learning, and trust—a policy containing rational methods of cleaning up transgressions or violations of agreements. The application of the concepts in this book will go a long way toward this type of achievement in a relationship.

How to Make a Man

Earlier we talked about Agreement versus Compromise. I made a distinction that matters of integrity could only be changed by agreement. Matters of procedure could be compromised upon. "Do not try to change the man," we hear often. There are things you can do to guide him toward being a better man, but you must keep in mind that you are only trying to help him gain his integrity. It is neither your responsibility nor your right to change him, but to help him recognize, tap into and live up to his already existing principles that make up who he is. Help him to blossom. Stand by him and remain truthful and honest.

He will agree to make a change in this direction, because it involves his own sanity, his own pride, and the ability to look in the mirror and be glad to be the person he is. But will he see it?

Once you, as a woman, know how to actively establish and enhance your own integrity, you will acquire the strength and certainty to enforce it in him.

I intentionally use the word enforce because it requires the force of will to demand and insist that he make himself whole—to understand his principles and live by them. A man has to create and live his own integrity, but when he has not completely done so, you can play the role of his gentle guide. A woman is very powerful and can turn a humanoid male into a Man!

How? Get him to list his principles. Discuss the principles he lives by and the principles he believes in but finds he is not able to live up to for one reason or another. This conversation alone will go a long way toward getting him to understand that when he compromises his principles he is disintegrating, and not living up to his full potential.

He is of no use to himself or to you if he compromises his principles. By doing so he is unwittingly betraying you, and your trust in him will suffer. You cannot stand by a man who does not stand up for what he believes. Point this out to him. This will get him on his toes, and he will work himself right in short order.

You must also be prepared to accept the fact that he might be so corrupt that he has massive internal conflicts, and may not even know what his principles are or how to identify the ones that he does have. He may live by double standards—convenient rules to apply at times, and discard at others. This is a more difficult raw material from which to make a man. If you come across one of these, think seriously before undertaking such a task.

If you choose to fall in love with such man, your job is ever so much more difficult. Here is where you can fully apply the information provided in the conflict resolution section to get him to dissect and re-evaluate things for himself. If you do it carefully and still allow him to be right, your success is assured. Of course, there is probably excess baggage from his past that sometimes requires healing, but even healing won't happen without integrity.

Let me stress again, you are not changing anything else about him except to get him to live his principles. Nothing else! Not his personality, not his habits, not his etiquette, not anything else!

Love is a fruit in season at all times,
and within the reach of every hand.
~ Mother Teresa ~

Chapter Twelve
Charting A Course

Part of growing up involves the process of defining and redefining objectives and goals. As we acquire more knowledge these things change. What then would be rational approach to defining our objectives when we are young if the very process of life is one of continuous redefinition?

It may not be rational to demand of oneself such well-defined objectives from the start. Nevertheless, to support the ongoing activity of achieving ever-increasing clarity of definition, the acquisition of knowledge and wisdom should be an underlying objective. Knowledge and wisdom are acquired through conscientious observation, study and contemplation.

We've experienced a wide variety of general objectives in our travels from one life stage to another. There are also objectives implied by behavior, that is, the things a person is currently doing are the expression of objectives, although not always clearly defined.

The objective of marriage can itself have any number of other hidden, personal objectives: production of off-spring, emotional support, sexual pleasure, company for social affairs, avoidance of loneliness, economic stability, friendship, someone to grow old with.
We asserted that a set of rigid rules for all objectives is irrational. Each set of circumstances requires different behaviors and responses.

We were educated to believe that marriage, as a loftier and broader objective, resolved many personal objectives. This may have been true at various points in time, when personal objectives were prevalently similar and relatively stable. Economic and social stability, and widely held ideological agreements, left little to be considered in establishing a relationship beyond whether the individuals liked each other and appeared relatively compatible.

In our times, there is extensive worldwide communication and a broad spectrum of cultural, ideological, and economic variances, even within the culture of a small community. In this setting, liking alone is a very limited criterion.

Earlier in our western culture, prior to the mid 20th century, our grandparents, and great grandparents met between the ages of 16 to 19. They went to the same churches and schools, read the same books, were in the same social circles, and had parents with similar ideologies and morals which were passed on. They were in a similar social and economic environment and understood and agreed on just about everything. They experienced the same stresses from economic depressions, fought the same battles and won the same victories. They had clearly defined roles. They had an average of about eight children. Their relationships were very loving, lasting into the late years of their lives. We wonder how we could possibly have such a loving union, when we see our own parents living an entirely different life:

Closer to the present, post-mid 20th century, our parents married in their 20's, had three children, came from different communities, had gone to different universities, were members of different religious groups, belong to different political ideologies, had a wonderful romance for the first two years of their marriage, and divorced within the first 15 years. They remarried and gave us half brothers and half sisters.

Our post-mid 20th century parents did not leave us much of a legacy with which to manage our connections. They left us to fend for ourselves, to arrive at our own solutions in coping with relationships and connections. And we loved and love them dearly and eventually forgave and overlooked their shortcomings when we arrived at our 40's and 50's, realizing the magnitude of their struggles. (I'm not precisely referring to specific parents, as I am to the parents of the family styles just described.)

It is no wonder that many educators and leaders want us to go back a hundred years and replay the rules that worked; they call it: Going back to basics. The rules worked because they evolved around the social environment of that time.

It is my premise that it is ever so much more rational to understand any given current environment and adjust our rules and behavior accordingly. Why should we not consider new ways of dealing with connections and relationships and other social constructs? History shows us how the structure of families and social groups varies according to economics and social events of the times; they were not necessarily governed by rigid rules that were applicable for all time, forever.

There was a time when families had several mothers per family, when populations were scarce and the natural progression of the species required higher levels of reproductive activity. At other times, in some cultures where food and resources were scarce, in order to mitigate a population explosion, economic and social conditions required fewer mothers, fewer children and more than one father per family. Some of our cultures have no provisions for such adjustments, but there have been times in our history when having more than one partner was considered not only normal, but also necessary.

Such ideas, morally or socially incorrect as they might appear in our culture today, must come to the forefront and be taken into consideration, among any other ideas yet undiscovered, which will enhance and protect the survival of the individual, the species, and the environment in which they dwell.

How can you view your own objectives nested in such volatile foundation?

Let's assume you are seeking a more profound involvement with someone. Do you have a clear idea of what that consists of? Imagine what a typical month of this new, profound relationship would look like?

Actions reflect intentions held in the mind. When actions don't give a clear idea of what's in the mind, then it is a fair assumption that there are no clear objectives or intentions. Heading into a serious relationship with someone who has not established objectives is walking on shaky ground. You never know what you are really getting into. It could be a world of adventure, misadventure, opportunity, lost opportunities, and uncertainties. It is not necessarily an evil world, but you should know that is the world you are entering when you decide you want a stronger commitment, but have no clear idea as to what that represents. You should recognize that there are risks, and understand that upon entering that world without a clear idea of your objectives, you are declaring your acceptance of the potential mysteries and risks. You will likely walk into things you had not expected, not the least of which is falling into the role of becoming merely a sexual partner.

You say, and not unlike other women, "If I were to know that he did want to commit to me right now, I probably would not hold back on sex. But since I still have a lot to figure out and only time can expose these kinds of answers, I am going to wait and see what he wants to do. I know that he wants sex; I am not trying to fool myself into thinking that he doesn't. It is normal for him to feel this way. I just want him to really understand that I DON'T and WON'T sleep with just anyone, regardless of how attracted I am to him. It would take more from him to get me to go in that direction."

You must understand the reasons you have for maintaining given connections. Having clear ideas about your feelings and your needs is a key to your success in starting, developing and nurturing connections. Granted, it is difficult to always see clearly, much less explain your own needs to yourself; therefore, taking action becomes difficult.

There are no hard and fast rules that are applicable at all times, as I mentioned earlier. They often depend on your personal objectives—that is to say, the result you wish to achieve. Consider defining and redefining your needs and

Chapter Twelve — Charting a Course

objectives regularly. This is an important process which will not only allow you to recognize actions to take in response to given circumstances, but will also put you in touch with yourself.

Maybe your objective reads something like this: I want this person because I have a feeling of need. This is a common objective. But you should always seek to refine such vague objectives in order to discover more easily obtainable goals.

What do you really want that you feel such need? Do you simply need a feeling of being connected to someone? Do you need a sexual partner? Do you need the feeling of comfort in someone else's words toward you? Are you seeking the need or experience of being loved? What does your concept of being loved really consist of? What will satisfy you? Are you expecting certain actions from him in order to understand whether you have what you need? What could these actions be? What is the reassurance you are seeking?

Ask yourself these questions in order to help define and refine your understanding of your needs and objectives. The clearer these objectives are, the easier it is to understand what actions you must take to obtain a desired result. Understanding and defining these things for yourself will go a long way toward establishing the certainty you need in deciding how you want the connection to grow.

A More Adventurous Life

There is, however, another way to conduct your life. We seem to be in a society that continuously suggests we should be well structured and clearly focused on what our needs and objectives are. Yet, it is not by decree of the wisdom of the universe that such should be the case. Life can be quite an adventure when one exposes oneself to the roulette of uncertainty. Is it necessary that I have a well-structured path? At present, the current carries me where it will, and I like it better. I'm taken to places I wouldn't have gone if I had followed some well-structured plan, with neatly defined objectives.

Most people lead this kind of life by default. They simply allow things to flow as they may and sit on the side of the road waiting for incredible opportunities. Does this pay off? If you like the process and enjoy what you get from it, that's the payoff. How do you make it pay off? Living such a style of life is so unpredictable that it's impossible to attempt a set of rules of the road. You make the rules as you go along. What worked today will not necessarily work tomorrow. You make it pay off by seizing the opportunities as they come along and letting your fears fall by the wayside.

Much of the outcome of such a lifestyle depends greatly on luck, often created by a positive attitude and general outlook, which tend to put us in places and circumstances that turn out fortuitous. It also requires launching oneself into new worlds and situations almost continuously, exposing oneself to new and unusual situations.

What would that style of life look like? It is a spontaneous reaction or pro-action with regard to situations and circumstances? Imagine going out to dinner with friends. On your way you see a wedding in progress. You stop the car and join the wedding party. You smile at all the relatives and simply answer, when asked, "I'm a friend of the other side." This is a spontaneous change towards a routine that we rarely practice; yet it can bring fascinating turns of events which will create repercussions in other areas of life, sometimes immediate, sometimes visible years later.

Once, as I got up from my work desk, I suddenly had the idea that this Halloween I would go to a party. That evening as I went for my walk, I simply walked, uninvited, into a party in a very private, plush side of town. The host, and owner of the property, was at the door. I approached him, shook his hand and greeted him as if he should know me. (For some mysterious reason, he was being rather dense and refused to recognize me.) I hugged him and gave him a kiss as one would an old friend, and said, "We'll have to sit down later and have a drink for old time sake." The host was busy and didn't have a chance to sit with me until the party was winding down. We sat and chatted while he desperately tried to remember where and when we had met. After a few minutes of this silly banter, I simply told him, "I'm just someone who walked in from the street; I have crashed your party." At first, he turned pale, then, in the next moment, he burst out laughing. He then shook my hand vigorously and hugged me, and told me how he admired my guts, especially in the presence of the two husky bouncers who had already dispatched a couple of other crashers.

Well, the point of this story is to show how such events can impact you life in unexpected ways. Ten years later, I found myself sitting in his country home in Costa Rica enjoying some cool summer drinks and relishing the friendship we had marginally maintained all those years.

It is up to you; adventure can pay off sometimes if it helps you acquire wisdom and connections.

A Matter of Balance

No hard and fast rule can be applied in all circumstances of life successfully, as I've reiterated several times. It is necessary to understand what the effect will be upon the ultimate objective if a rule is shifted or altered.

For example, many people maintain their connections by certain routine actions that involve periodic contacts, such as the monthly phone call or the yearly greeting card. In other words, the continued existence of that connection is totally dependent upon this periodic contact. If it were to stop, the connection would break. You might ask, "Why maintain a connection if the other side would simply abandon the contact, if they were not prompted to respond or stay in contact?" Each of us has purposes and objectives that motivate us.

Maintaining such connections obviously satisfies some objective, whether we know what the objective is or not.

You are doing something similar; you find yourself waiting for a long time to hear from someone. Let us assume for a moment that the interest at the other end is not sufficient to cause him to reach out to you. You then initiate the reach yourself, again and again, for as long as you wish to maintain that connection. In such a case, you must consider whether you wish to sustain the repeated links, and whether you are comfortable with the idea that the connection exists because of your periodic contacts.

There is nothing wrong with that, assuming you know that you are doing it and why you are doing it, and you are willing to have it continue that way. Now, if you chose to apply that approach to sustain an intimate connection, you might need to decide if you want the other person show his commitment to the existence of the connection by initiating contacts. Also, you have to decide whether some expression of commitment is present during those times when you are together. If there is an adequate show of interest, you may choose to take on the responsibility of the periodic reaches to keep the connection alive.

Pursuing people in this fashion can be perceived as humiliating. "He doesn't care about me, and is just being polite by responding, which he does only when I call him." But you don't have to pay attention to what others will think. The idea is to keep a connection open with someone you feel has a positive role in your life.

This maintenance of the connection, the times you spend together, will have the additional effect of becoming somewhat of a habit in their lives. Eventually it will not be difficult for the other person take some responsibility for their feelings and actions. They may begin reaching to you of their own accord.

A woman friend, Rita, recently told me about a wonderful experience she had involving another woman, let's caller Julia, she met at a party. My friend thought Julia was a bit too different from the type of associations she was accustomed to. So Rita did not return phone calls, and on one occasion did not answer the door when Julia stopped by. Julia seemed almost desperate to talk to Rita. Eventually, Rita gave in, and began chatting with Julia. Through many subsequent chats they discovered many common ideas and realities and became very good friends. That was twenty years ago, and today they remain close friends.

People with initiative make things happen. People without it get swept in the direction of the initiative of others. Your choice is whether you want to manage someone or find someone with more or less equal level of initiative.

Beware that in your avoidance of people you are allowing what could be a weakness to develop. Whether it is a weakness is not as important as whether you feel comfortable being the one with the initiative. It may be a major character difference between you and your potential partner, which later on could potentially stress the connection. This difference may not disturb you at all, and to you it may not be a critical element to the connection. You have to decide whether you can live with what may be an extreme difference between both of you.

In the final analysis, if you are making a one-sided effort to maintain the connection, do so understanding the risks, and be willing to take them. Don't show apprehension or concern. You're simply staying in touch because you like him, and you're the type of person that likes to stay in touch with your friends. You enjoy his company from time to time, and you're simply staying in touch. There is no other reason for calling. There really shouldn't be.

Conversely, you might consider why you chose to pursue someone who doesn't put forth the same effort, when it is less difficult to accept the advances of someone who already has a strong interest in you. It's a matter of balance between what you have to work with and what you want!

Shadows From the Past–The Return of Old Lovers

There is an interesting phenomenon that I've seen take place around the time people begin making closer ties, and there exists the possibility of establishing commitments.

I have observed and confirmed through observation (with an uncanny degree of frequency) that old lovers return, and they often return right around the time a major change is about to take place in your life. As a life event, this may not seem terribly significant, but upon closer observation there appear to be some noteworthy patterns.

It is a human characteristic not to want to fail. In the face of real or imagined failure the individual makes a mental note for future action on a possible recovery from such failure. It seems that the intention to win continues past the apparent irreparable state of affairs, with an uncanny tenacity.

The following scenario reveals a specific pattern which occurs in most such events that involve the return of an old lover:

You have recently met someone that seems to have good potential for the connection you wanted to create. After spending time getting to know each other, in his mind, he begins to contemplate the possibility of making a stronger commitment toward, let's say, the next stage of the connection. Out of nowhere comes an old lover. In spite of his developing feelings for you, he goes out with her once or twice, and suddenly you receive an announcement that they have decided to give the old connection another try.

If it has come to this point, the message you receive tells you that you may not have made a deep enough impression to enable him to clearly distinguish you as being a better potential partner than his old flame. You have no choice except to bow out gracefully, congratulating him on his good fortune and wishing him well. My challenge to you is to do your best to maintain, from this point forward, a friendly periodic contact with him. Remember that a large pool of potential contacts is always useful. He might even be instrumental in connecting you to someone more ready for you than he was.

How did this happen? Remember the underlying intention not to lose? This might immediately sound like a ridiculous idea, but let's keep our minds open and explore the possibilities. I imagine and suspect that on some level there is a connection between the old lovers that signals the potential

Chapter Twelve — Charting a Course

of the last opportunity to make the failed connection work. Don't blame yourself for this event. While it's not something that will happen every time, I have seen it happen enough to constitute a pattern to which one should pay attention.

That they want to try it again is a valiant effort. They deserve the credit. If they rebuild their connection with more care, using healthy ingredients, there is a chance they can win. If they don't, they will follow the road of most of the retries. A fairly large percentage of retries do fail, for the very same reason they failed the first time. Don't make this a reason to hang around waiting for the second break to occur. Move on and open new ground while keeping the line of friendship open.

If on the other hand, the old lover shows up after commitments have been made, you have an entirely new issue on your hand. There are many elements involved, including personal integrity, betrayal, hidden motives, and much more, especially if your connection he is now beginning to look back, nostalgically, and starts taking actions to prompt or allow a reunion with the past lover.

Because of the many possible issues, you should be familiar with this entire book to understand what issue has come to the forefront in your connection, and how to handle it.

Shoals and narrows are areas at sea where a ship can become bogged on sand banks or crash against the proverbial rocks. This is pure conflict, and simply stated, it is an idea versus another, an intention or action versus another, both acting at once, usually with equal force, therefore frozen in the collision.

Part IV
The Shoals and Narrows

Since love grows within you, so beauty grows.
For love is the beauty of the soul.
~ St. Augustine ~

Chapter Thirteen
Inner Conflict

The first area where conflict must be resolved is inside oneself. Inner conflict arises out of our own natural impulses, or other acquired and accepted realities, coming up against external social, religious, moral and political conditioning, which have been internalized (taken in as forces to be accepted). It is a continuous battle that rages within, wherein one can perceive impulses and desires, which at the same time must be restrained, because they fly up against the face of social acceptability, customs and traditions. The conditioning is so deeply imbedded that most people truly consider most conditioned behavior natural.

Usually we tend to follow the style and actions of our peers. Having had little or no formal instruction in the process of creating connections, we have no other sources outside our parents, and our peers. Our parents are not at the stage where we are; they are not just coming together or just beginning to learn about each other. In this particular area, there's little to gain from them by way of example, because their example is not applicable to our lives. Therefore, unless we get direct instruction from them, the bulk of our information comes from older peers.

Those very peers are in the identical situation we are. So the question arises, how did they learn and where did they learn? Tradition and conditioning! Tradition is conditioning. Whether this is immediately believable or not is unimportant. What is important at this moment is the distinction, or at least the concept of a distinction, between our own natural tendencies as human creatures and that which we have been trained to accept as the proper behavior. What makes it important now is that we are at a stage where we are called upon to evolve beyond the traditions and conditionings presented to us. Why the need for this? There would not be any need to ask such a question if we simply observe the world around us. I am challenging you to review the traditions you have been raised with, and compare them to other possibilities. What new concepts and ideas might be more natural, more rational, and ultimately more workable with regard to your future?

The process of integrating these conflicting ideas comes next. It can be a lifetime task. Integration refers to the reconciliation (or bringing into agreement) between your inner natural impulses, the ideas you have acquired from learning, and many of the social realities to which you have been exposed. In other words, the ideas that appear to be in conflict, and your desires, that seem to be contrary to what you are told, must fit together and make sense. This is a very natural growth process.

Education is a process of exposure to new ideas which then need to be weeded through for what is valid and what is not, and included as part of your reality. If the new idea to which you are exposed is contrary to what you already believe, it will generate inner conflict. The process of reconciling these differences lies in your ability to resolve truths. Ah! Truth! What is truth?

Look over your own life and find areas where you acted with complete confidence. Seek out those areas where you were sure that you knew what you were doing. Now, try to locate an area where you were somewhat uncertain. This may be difficult to do because you are accustomed to avoid initiative in areas you have failed to act with confidence in the past. Review and compare both areas. As you review each area, look for elements that connect you to the area of confidence and elements that connect you to the area of uncertainty. Those elements can be found by answering the question (or variations thereof), "What about this area makes me so confident/

Chapter Thirteen — Inner Conflict

uncertain?" Notice that the underlying principles in the area of greater certainty are quite clear to you. Do those principles make a great deal of sense? Do they easily relate to the reality you had the time you acted with complete confidence?

Now review the basic concepts and principles of the areas of lesser certainty. Are they somewhat vague and unclear? Do you have trouble making sense of them?

In order to achieve inner integration you can see the strengths that lie in your personal awareness of truth—the truth you observe and perceive through your senses and your spiritual awareness. It is not what someone else said it is; it's what you discover through your own observation.

To resolve inner conflict you have to review currently held truths that appear to be in conflict. Once you have listed those ideas, you can ask these questions of each one:

* Where and when did I ever get this idea?
* Who did I admire or love or respect that advanced the idea?
* Mentally review the conversation in which the idea was first presented to you, and how you came to accept it as true.
* How can this idea be true/not be true?
* How did my life work because I applied this idea?
* Do I have a special interest for it to be this way?
* What would I lose something if I discover this to be true (or false)?
* Allow yourself the same respect or love that you held for the person that gave you the idea in the first place.
* Review the idea in the present and decide anew whether it's a valid idea or not, and allow yourself to create a new idea if you need one.

Ask the questions of each side of the conflict, first one side, and then the other. Use the drill to look within your heart and mind to reach new understandings.

External Conflict

Conflicts are disagreements which become apparent when actions in daily life are affected by opposing ideas. If there are disagreements or differences in ideologies that do not touch daily activities of life, they rarely surface as conflicts.

Conflicts are unavoidable. They can be devastating to connections when they are not resolved. When a conflict fails to resolve through the participant's usual style, role-playing can be a useful first step.

Role-playing is a fairly standard and successful method of resolving conflicts. It's when two or more people act out a given conflict, and experience the process of resolving it. It can be followed by a reversal of roles, and again, an attempt at resolution. It is easier to temper one's emotions in a dry run than to try to practice it for the first time right in the middle of the first conflict!

You can practice these processes with a friend, a relative or just about anyone. If you already have had to deal with conflict, you understand that knowing how to do it before applying it is better than feeling your way through it in the actual experience of a fight!

There are several elements that must be emphasized and understood for conflict resolution to work at all:
1) The method or system of communication.
2) Willingness to allow the possibility that your partner is right.
3) Recognition of the issues.
4) Freedom from Guilt.

The last three points are not well understood in drills I have observed used for role-playing. If these elements are not understood, role playing and real conflict resolution become meaningless.

Step One - Communication Methods

Establish and agree upon a method of presenting the issues to one another. A fairly acceptable way of doing this is by taking turns at exposing some components of your concerns, taking care not to interrupt each other too much or break the train of thought. Too many interruptions tend to cause one to forget, resulting in the inability to clearly convey the messages in question.

Mentally break down an issue into smaller components, so you can present small, but complete information. Ensure that presentations that are not so extensive that they cause the other side to loose attention or interest. As you have opportunities to engage in the practice of conflict resolution, you will establish, by practice, what is too much or too little information. Sometimes when the amount of material is too extensive, it is fair to suspect that more than one issue is at play.

Step Two - Willingness to Grant Rightness

In attempting to resolve conflicts it is necessary to allow the possibility that the other person is right. To accomplish this it is necessary to consider the point and examine the reasons why it might be right, making an honest effort to see the rightness of the other side.

The previous step is a matter of procedure. This step is a matter of discernment and observation. No resolution will occur if this step is missing. It is generally the inability to entertain the possibility that the other person is right which causes resolution attempts to fail, arguments and fights to repeat themselves like recordings, creating greater and greater intolerance, deeper and deeper disappointments, larger and larger chasms between sides, and finally, departure and withdrawal of affection. If you are willing to see both sides to issues, you will survive any errors in the other two steps.

Step Three - Recognition of Issues

This is the most difficult part of conflict resolution. Let's review it by illustrating a hypothetical event.

You come home at midnight and find your front door locked. Another internal lock has bet set by hand. After some forceful pounding, your partner finally opens the door and says: "that'll teach you for coming at this late hour."

That statement is followed by an argument where you go on for half an hour explaining why you had the right to stay out as long as you wanted and come home at whatever time you wished. You also give very convincing evidence that clearly justifies your being late. Finally your friend agrees your reason for being late is valid, and agrees not to do it again. Two weeks later the same thing repeats itself.

It is obvious that the conflict did not completely resolve during the first round of discussions. Why? A basic issue has been overlooked: Should or should not the door be locked to prevent your entrance, regardless of reason for doing so? Once this issue is resolved the conflict never reoccurs.

A resolved issue contains certain obvious elements that include agreement on the philosophy or principle at play and agreement on what is acceptable action for the particular type of event.

Non-Issues

Joanne has known Christopher for sometime, and between them there is a very good foundation of conflict resolution. One day Chris shows up with a solemn attitude. Pressed for a reason he finally complains that he's been feeling neglected; that Joanne spends too much time at work. Joanne is stunned since her work schedule has been essentially the same since they met. Believing Chris has a valid concern, she spends some time trying to understand and propose very viable changes. Chris finds her proposals acceptable, but seems to linger in the somber mood and continues protesting mildly about the numerous times in the past that he had to change plans and accommodate her schedule changes.

Joanne off-handedly asked, "Hey! What happened that made you realize that you had problem with my work habits?" Chris pauses, and with a bit of embarrassment responds, "Marisa called me and asked me out, that last time you changed our date. We went for a coffee."

Joanne said, "Ah! You thought you did something wrong!" Chris admitted it, his mood changed, and the issue vanished.

A synthetic issue (non-issue!) was presented to justify an act Chris thought was a transgression to his agreements with Joanne. In our story the conflict resolved. If Chris had not taken responsibility for his act, it would have become the seed to their eventual break up. This mechanism of apparently insoluble issues is covered at a greater length in later sections dealing with break ups.

Step Four - Hidden Issues

Because people act based on behavior standards they often believe is given, agreed upon, and understood, they tend to gloss over points contained within a conflict, which prevent the conflict from resolving. Here is an example of the idea that everybody-knows that would never come up because people don't realize there is anything wrong with it. Normally the issue would have remained hidden, and the conflict, unresolved.

Cynthia was kicked out of a club meeting because, according to the moderator, she used profane language and was rude to others. When she argued that there was no basis for the removal, she was physically removed.

Cynthia filed a written complaint with Robert, the program manager, who told Cynthia not to be worry, and return to the next meeting. Cynthia insisted on a public apology and acknowledgement of the injustice.

Robert promised Cynthia he would read the transcripts, after which he told her he would take no further action, again advising her to return next meeting as if nothing had happened. Cynthia rejected the idea, and after further discussion, Robert made a very revealing statement, "If you were expelled, there must have been a sufficiently good reason for it." Robert was operating under the dubious assumption that a just cause was implied in the mere administration of punishment, and this assumption totally dismissed Cynthia's issues. To her there was the additional issue of the contents of her speech.

The off-hand dismissals, and everybody-knows assumptions are a very clear indication of hidden issues. It's time to dissect the apparent single issue into smaller and smaller components until each is clearly resolved.
Underlying false assumptions are trained-in patterns in maintaining a subtle moral hierarchy of behavior. Let me break it down further.

Rocking the Boat

Robert told Cynthia to return to the forum adding, "Don't rock the boat." The "deserved punishment, with its implied violation" and "don't rock the boat" are accepted attitudes of conventional wisdom. They have the effect of educating one into tolerating small injustices as normal expediencies. They are the unwritten rules and the source of the hidden, unresolved conflicts so long as they are not confronted directly.

Cynthia was able to pinpoint the sub-issues or hidden issues, at which point the use of conflict resolutions techniques could work. Robert promoted Cynthia to Moderator. The promotion served as the public apology and acknowledgement of the injustice.

When people allow themselves to be victims of small injustices because taking a stand becomes too costly, they risk the added potential of being further targeted, or may bring ridicule for fighting petty issues. They become accustomed to accept and overlook small injustices, thereby opening the door to more and more gradually introduced injustices. A few years of that cowardly attitude will give our children a society where they themselves will be slaves of an accumulation of injustices which will have come to be accepted as normal. Is that a worthwhile price to pay to avoid the discomfort of standing on a just principle?

Challenge and with each challenge, cross items off the unwritten rule list!

Freedom From Guilt

This is the last step in providing a new operating ground as part of conflict resolution. That ground must be clean of recriminations for wrong-doings.

Conflicts can start before an actual event or action that might constitute a breach has taken place, merely on the contemplation of an action to be taken. This is fairly easy to resolve at the time the person about to take action has announced it. Since the action has not yet taken place, it is not likely to be accompanied by any great emotional explosions, and can be negotiated before the fact—that is to say, before an agreement is ever breached. For example, Mike announces he's going to meet an old girlfriend after work. Martha is shocked at the idea. It is something she never expected. This can be source for conflict, but the announcement brings the potential conflict to the fore. Discussion reveals different standards each had before they came together. Now they have the opportunity to negotiate a way of dealing with such situations. On the other hand, conflicts do suddenly explode after an event has taken place. Previously unrecognized conflicts in reality can surface as the result of an action that makes the reality breach visible.

Consider first the severity of the breach, and second, the nature of the breach and its reconciliation.

These breaches are often met with explosive emotional reactions. It should be clear to the parties involved that such emotional explosions are often intended as an assertion of the severity of the act. Nevertheless it should not be accepted as an indicator of how bad the breach may have been or whether a breach has even taken place. All that can be said is that it is that a breach of reality has taken place. In other words, the action of one party did not fall within the reality of acceptable behavior of the other.

It is not uncommon that the participants in a social connection will bring their own set of rules and conditions, often assuming the other has the same rules, which is far from the truth.

It is important to differentiate between the severity of the breach and the emotional reaction to it. The volume of the anger is not directly proportional to the badness of the action. The anger only speaks for the state of mind of the angry party, and the unwillingness to accept or consider accepting the other's action, acting on a rule established in the mind, not necessarily a rule that applies to others. The anger is a separate issue than the breach of reality. It needs to be addressed separately, either before the breach of reality or immediately after. It is important to remove any lingering emotional debris because it becomes a means to enforce guilt upon either party.

Here are the steps to remove emotional debris from resolved conflict. Each participant, preferably in private, and specifically not with or in the presence of the other:

*Take a personal evaluation of your actions with regard to the conflict, and determine your responsibility. This is simply an awareness of the actions you have taken, devoid of excuses or reasons for taking them. It is the simple admission of having taken the action.

* Evaluate any harm done.
* Be willing to forgive yourself and all others in that scene.
* If the damage is severe and clear to all, recommend ideas for repair or any reasonable handling.

Finally, remember what we discussed in the section The Hidden, Dark Self. Consider the possibility that a highly explosive reaction to the acts of others reveals your own dark side. Take an honest look at the negative thoughts you have about others, and you are sure to see things about yourself that you wish to change

The greatest tragedy of life is not that men perish,
but that they cease to love.
~ W. Somerset Maugham ~

Chapter Fourteen
Helen, the Face that Launched a Thousand Ships

Helen of Troy is the legendary woman who captured the hearts of men, and over whose beauty and love wars were fought and lives were won and lost. She abandoned her husband, Menelaus, for the love of Paris, and ten years later returned to Menelaus. (There is much conflict between historical accounts as to what actually took place.) I use Helen as a metaphor for a special feature in love connections. When a strong attraction appears to take place only one way, it appears the channel which has opened is only flowing in one direction. That's how it looks between Helen and her men.
There is a Helen in some women, and there are the men who fall for her; this shows in a continuous pattern. There is a Helen in every woman at some point in her life. The features can appear also in men, but social paradigms make it less visible. Furthermore, I, being a man, choose to write it from a man's point of view.

Helen, you have an irresistible allure. Men fall over themselves to win your favors, and when they're irresistibly under your control, you seem to loose interest, and then you withdraw. There is a trail of broken hearts in your wake, and you are at a loss to understand why or how to avoid it. You are the woman about whom stories of love, passion and violence are written. You have the power of love.

Your outgoing and ever-flowing love and lust for life is infectious, and people simply gravitate to you. This is a most delicious state of affairs. You are in power, and you enjoy it.

But there is one big danger which continues to plague you. Those for whom you have the greatest initial attraction will nearly always become obsessed with you. And almost as invariably, it is YOU who initiates the reach. And the obsession will alternate back and forth.

A lifetime of observation strongly supports the idea that a fearless, outgoing, and loving outreach is a natural quality to all humans. This is especially visible during the childhood years. Life, training, stress, indoctrination, education and other pressures cause most people to restrain their natural outreach and curiosity. You have retained the natural outgoing characteristic. This makes you easily attractive, because your show of interest and curiosity in others draws them to you.

Most visible to others is the way in which you overwhelm your lovers with the flow of natural allure, love, lust, curiosity, interest, and passion that emanate from you. You may not feel you have this ability, but your outgoing nature sends out vibrations. Your childhood curiosity is now seeking experiences in other areas of life.

Those who respond to your call, and follow cadence to the step and rhythm of your allure and passion, will become obsessed with you. You will know who these people are, because you will also feel drawn by them. You had that special feeling the instant you saw them. You know that they had the very same feeling, because you felt it.

While this type of connection has the makings of a truly wonderful union, it can very easily turn into a nightmare. You can make the difference in the way you approach the connection in all its aspects. There is no special set of instructions that apply to you exclusively. All of the things that have been discussed in this book will be very useful. The important thing is that you must fill in all of the other ingredients we discussed: the gradual communication, the exploration and creation of common realities, the understanding of objectives. But above all, you have to allow the passionate side to advance no faster than all the other elements. The problem is your lover's assumption that you will give yourself to him in a way you cannot give yourself to him. You will always flow freely outwardly, and will enjoy seeing and meeting people. You want him as your mate, but you don't want him to have you on the exclusive level you assume he expects. Your loving and outgoing characteristics can become a source of jealousy to your partner; if so, there will be very unpleasant consequences.

You heart is purely delicious, and when a man insists on making you his exclusive possession, and you allow it according to your reasoning, you are both lost. You will begin to experience his obsession for you if his feelings have arrived at that point where he wants to make you his. You probably have gone too far, too fast, without filling in all the intervening components.

There are many ways of dealing with your alluring nature, but you may think that becoming the exclusive mate to one man is not one of them. You will have to know and understand how to allow yourself to flow unrestricted, while you accomplish the other objectives of your life. At different times of life, you will need and appreciate different things.

Drawn by Passion

When the channel first opened, it did indeed flow in both directions, but Helen pulled back, she withdrew. Her reach may have been innocent and gentle, and her withdrawal may have been just as casual and gentle, as if it had been understood the reach was perhaps somewhat insignificant. Suddenly she finds herself assailed by an obsessed lover. This can happen occasionally to anyone, but to Helen it is a repetitive pattern, a problem to her, and her lovers.

Every one of Helen's lovers is absolutely sure that what he is experiencing is a love of the highest and purest nature. The power of its bond is unbreakable, the thirst for the constant contact, insatiable.

Obsession! The word has a Latin origin, from the basic form 'ob' near, and 'sedeo' sit. This translates to 'staying put,' or 'surrounding as in a siege,' 'feeling compelled to remain.' The dictionary says: Compulsion, irrational motives, irrational impulse: a strong spontaneous and irrational motivation. Another associated meaning: fixation or unhealthy preoccupation with something or someone. Also, preoccupation: an idea that preoccupies the mind and holds the attention. Common usage tends to suggest a nuance of futility.

Many of the words in the above definition make the concept very confusing because their meanings are abstract, and their nuances vary from one person to the next, thus, are highly subjective. The root meaning carries a clearer idea of the concept. All the ideas conveyed by the words in the standard definition can be distorted by the intensity implied by the writer or assumed by the reader. How illogical, irrational, fixated, or unhealthy can an impulse be, to be considered an obsession? It can go quite far, even into violence, if the obsession is not curbed or requited!

For our purpose, here is a workable, clear distinction so we are able to recognize what we are attempting to manage. Obsession is accompanied by almost continuous apprehension and undesirable feelings, including fear of loss, and suspicion. These feelings tend to cause serious distractions and neglect in other areas of life for which the person would otherwise take responsibility.

Love, on the other hand, is generally accompanied by joy, greater productivity, feelings of emotional security, and some measure of happiness, if one can envision one's objectives being accomplished. Obsession (the sensation of being irresistibly drawn) can also be labeled love. The difference can be purely subjective; whereas two people feeling the exact same thing would use either word (love or obsession) to describe it. I point out distinctly different symptoms to show the difference between obsession and love. These distinctions provide an easy way to identify each according to meaningfully different symptoms, since attempting to treat love as an obsession, or an obsession as love, will produce undesirable results.

The irresistible attraction itself is not obsession. Notice the descriptive word futile in the definition above. The emotional tug-o-war is the important element that can convert an irresistible attraction into an obsession.

Early during the writing this book I found myself caught in a fast, fiery emotional connection, which, in no time at all, had me wrapped up in what I then denied as an obsession. I refused to believe I could be become a helpless victim of the dreaded obsession. I felt compelled to remove from the book some of the material that I had written at the time, believing that all I had written were rationalizations to vindicate my feelings. When the obsession ran its course, I reworked the materials and modified them to include some new understandings.

A Broader Concept of Obsession

My new observation made clear to me the mechanics of this interesting phenomenon, which gives us an expanded and clearer definition, and makes it possible to manage this form of energy in most cases.

Obsession takes place when one's energy is drawn into the vacuum left by a real, imagined, or feared withdrawal of affection (more broadly, anything withdrawn). Obsession can be seen as the feeling that follows being pulled toward something or someone. It is such an irresistible draw toward the object of the obsession that we can scarcely keep our attention from it. The object of an obsession can be anything toward which a person has an irresistible attraction. The individual feels energy or objects move away. This is very mechanical and follows the laws of physics. It leaves a vacuum in the space it occupied; the resulting vacuum draws into itself energy or objects from its surroundings.

Many people I interviewed believed they were the only ones obsessed, but upon interviewing the parties on the other side, it came to light that if there was love to begin with, the obsession is generally experienced by both sides. Both sides feel the emptiness and want to fill it with what is left.

The obsession began the instant something was withdrawn from his/her space. Energy has been withdrawn. Love has been withdrawn. Attention has been withdrawn. Expressions of caring were withdrawn. The physical body of the other person is gone. It feels like a huge loss. The withdrawal of energy created an energy vacuum. This vacuum exerts a great deal of force and draws energy; hence the pulled and drawn sensation, which is in fact the obsession.

The power of the obsession depends on the predisposition of the person experiencing it, and on various emotional factors prevailing in the connection at the time of the withdrawal.

Helen, as far as you know, there is nothing you do intentionally that causes others to become obsessed with you. You open the trap door to obsession by a sudden withdrawal of yourself, your love, and affection. At the moment you do that, a signal reaches the other end, and suddenly they feel the vacuum you have just created, into which all of their energies begin to drain. In fact, when they are pulled into the vacuum you left; their reaction is to try to pull you back to fill it. Now you experience just as sudden a pull back into the emptiness you left.

I've interviewed many who have experienced being obsessed over. One for one they assert they are not doing anything unusual. But when it is pointed out, they do in fact recognize the pattern of withdrawal and some level of intent behind it. It is not always visible because the outgoing behavior is quite natural. It looks the same as any other social reach, and is easily rationalized that way. The difference is that other social reaches are not responded to with the same effusiveness that you, Helen, emanate when you make the first reach, so you are baffled when certain emanations are returned in kind. This is what sets the pattern in motion.

An obsessed person needs to believe the motive is love. What else would justify such apparently insane behavior, and be excusable! And there is a great deal of love. There had to be to produce the obsession. That is one of the reasons the person has rationalized, and justified the behavior, which at other times would be unacceptable. But Love is neither the direct cause of the behavior nor the cause of the obsession. The withdrawal is.

Other schools of thought on obsession see it as a disease. When a person is obsessed, he can go to a medical doctor, and get antidepressant medication. It is often called manic-depressive. It is sometimes seen as an antisocial trait. It is viewed as a dangerous emotion to exhibit when courting or attempting to begin a relationship, and in many other social settings. If we are obsessed, we think we are exhibiting a weakness of character; and we hide the fact that we are afflicted with such a terrible disease.

In retrospect, I realize that the primary reason the nature of obsession, its mechanics, and cure were out of grasp was because those who have been victims of obsession have been so subjectively immersed that they are unable to see it clearly. Social ambivalence of acceptance/rejection of obsession also contributes to lack of understanding.

Warning Signs

Here are some not necessarily conclusive events that suggest you might be dealing with Helen!

You are sitting quietly in your room watching television. Suddenly you feel something from him, something disturbing, and something that doesn't feel quite right to you. You have the urge to call him right now! You call, and find his tone of voice somewhat different, possibly even a bit cool. He makes some excuse as to why he's not able to talk at this moment. You hang up, and now find yourself filled with apprehension, and cannot but become totally fixated on him. This is a mild form of obsession. This scenario is not uncommon. People seem to sense what is going on in the people they feel close to. Is it coincidence?

Another example:

You see a stranger across a crowded room, or anywhere, and you connect, and feel incredibly admired and loved. The person will tell you how you have so thoroughly won their heart. Over the next few days, you will experience amazement at the power of the connection and will begin to be drawn to this person. They will most likely seek your company and will go out of their way to be with you. You come to consider this person worthy of your attention and affection, and you begin to return the attention to some degree. The other person suddenly starts showing some confusion about the experienced feelings. They may reach strongly for reassurance or they may start withdrawing. A reach can be a signal that withdrawal is soon to follow, particularly if you sense apprehension. This is usually a fast and furious relationship; high fire; high stress, and high emotions.

Communications with Helen do not bring about any real resolution of ideas and realities. You are as uncertain about her ideas and beliefs as she claims uncertainty about yours. Her communication is scattered, and she often manages to avoid discussing your concerns. The incredible need to come to terms at a fast pace causes too many issues to be brought up, but never really understood. A flurry of strong sexual and emotional bond accompanies most of these signs. If you are caught amidst this emotional turmoil, you are at the onset of obsession. The exercises in the next section will help you unravel the situation.

Easing and Relieving Obsession

Your obsession is caused by Helen's withdrawal and rejection. Any attempts to persuade Helen to do otherwise will be futile at this time. Now focus on freeing yourself from the obsession as quickly as possible.

If your obsession is visible in your actions, Helen will reject you even more. Your friends and the society around you will often avoid you as well. You will be seen as an avalanche and they will run to avoid you.

The remedy is to pull oneself and one's energy back into oneself, back into one's space. We understand what the emotional event is; therefore we can do something about it. We know that something is being pulled from us into a vacuum.

I have already worked this drill with a number of people, and find it quite effective.

1. The recognition of the obsession, of course, is necessary. "Hmmm, I'm obsessed; or at least it seems I am being drawn, and I feel a bit out of control."

2. Establish exactly what has been removed or taken or has left your space; understand the something that has gone, and try to understand what is gone, and where it has gone! You can observe these things when you are sitting alone, anguishing over her. Her body is not next to you. You do not feel her touch; you look around and see images of things that are no longer there. All you are doing in this step is acknowledging what you perceive. It has to be done accurately.

3. Focus your attention on the space where your energy has gone, and on your immediate surroundings.

4. Physically, hold onto something large and solid where you are. Any object that's fixed and cannot be moved will work, like a doorway or a tree. Also hold on to the space mentally.

5. Get the sensation of pulling your energy from the space where it was drawn into. This mental exercise can be done in any way that works for you. Visualize the energy coming back into you. Get the feeling of pulling it, and the feeling that when you pull on it, it does come back. Imagine that you are pulling yourself and your energies back from that space, and see that it is happening.

6. Imagine something else, anything—flowers, sand, water—filling the vacuum, as you pull yourself away from it (If you are not currently suffering from obsession, and are trying to understand this entire process, you can create an

artificial feeling of obsession by getting the sensation of having something pulled from you. You can look around the room and take an object you love very much, and imagine it no longer there for a moment, and notice the anguish of the disappearance of that object. Then get the sensation that you are pulling it back from wherever you imagined the object went. This produces some clear sensations that you should be able to distinguish.)

    Do the drill. When you feel more relaxed, and you are fairly comfortable that the obsession has subsided, you can turn to deal with Helen again, who is quite possibly also suffering from an obsession that is pulling her away from you. The reasons she's pulling away can be better understood within the context of the entire cycle of a relationship and how it breaks down, covered later in The Wisdom Phase.

Chapter Fourteen

The Face of Helen

Romantic love is a passionate spiritual-emotional-
sexual attachment between a
man and a woman that reflects
a high regard for the value
of each other's person.
~ Nathaniel Branden ~

Chapter Fifteen
Violence and Abuse

Why should the topic of violence and abuse be included in this book? Violence and abuse is present in many relationships, and therefore, is worthy of much more than the few paragraphs. In your efforts to expand your life and establish connections, it is not unlikely that you will run into violence of one form or another. My purpose is to bring the matter to your consciousness, and to help you understand some of the basic concepts and minimal precautions that are within your immediate power.

Let's begin with a definition. Violence, violate, and the various words of similar root (vio) are derived from the Latin word Vis, meaning force. Force is a natural occurrence; it is found everywhere in nature. Motion is a basic attribute to all that exists; motion of any kind involves some level of force. To assume that all force is bad is as nonsensical as saying all force is good. An appropriate amount of force challenges the mind and/or the body and can subsequently generate an opportunity for learning. An inappropriate amount of force is likely to create overwhelm and become a barrier to learning. It can cause an individual to recoil in fear, or to assume a protective or defensive attitude.

In general usage, violence normally refers to inappropriate or excessive force, as seen by the victim, as opposed the source of the force. (What is good for the deer hunter is not necessarily good for the deer!) Life manifests in a variety of experiences, all containing some level of force. Criticism, lectures, scolding, warnings, threats, beatings, abuse, and even, to some degree, education and indoctrination—in essence, all experiences contain elements of force which press upon the conscience (or perhaps also the subconscious) of an individual to cause change.

Let us examine some aspects of abuse and violence that take place in relationships.

There is subtle violence, or abuse. Subtle violence reveals itself through words and is seemingly non-violent. This subtle violence can be as dangerous as physical violence, and its undesirable effects can last longer. Borrowing from our earlier definition, we can examine that there are actually more facets to violence than that which is typically acknowledged in our society.

Abuse, in addition to violence in the sense of our definition, implies the inability to take adequate or appropriate action to manage one's sphere of influence and control. A person believes that he or she has no effective way to deal with situations without exercising excessive force.

This takes the form of what can be called mental abuse:

Being lied to, deceived, misinformed, unjustly excluded, forcefully misguided or misinformed, yelled at, maliciously criticized, being made to feel guilty, being hounded, nagged, pressured to engage in certain actions, being rejected, forcefully advised or well-intentionally punished for your own good. There is also abuse in the form of absence of appropriate action, such as neglect, carelessness, indifference, abandonment, deprivation, absence or withdrawal of affection and nurturing. The list goes on.

Abuse is so widespread that if only half of what happens were aired, it would be quite apparent that there is hardly a person in this society that has been able to escape it. The victims do not tell for years, if ever, because they feel such intense confusion, guilt and shame. It is easy to find women, and even men, who have experienced one if not many instances of abuse, whether as adults or as children.

Sadly, the victims, blinded by their own dubious experiences, failed to notice that similar abuse was being committed by relatives or acquaintances against their own children, and are often shocked to discover it much too late to do anything about it.

What follows will make clear why so little ever comes to light.

Guilt and Abuse Fallout

To succeed in the execution of a task you must anticipate, understand and handle its principal obstacles. Guilt is one of the most prominent obstacles to success in many areas of life, including in the creation of meaningful connections. The victim's guilt in instances of abuse has surfaced as one of the principal barriers in the creation of meaningful connections.

Guilt will park your life right there on the spot for years, if not for the rest of your life. After more than thirty years of observation, I have come to recognize it as the most crippling disease in our society. The ravages of guilt are so abundant that it is often seen as a natural event of existence, rather than the plague it truly is.

Some of the more visible results of guilt are indecision and inaction, withdrawal, fear, unreasonable caution, loneliness, secrecy, remorse, inability to build happiness in life, inability to trust, and even disease and death ultimately resulting from heartache and heartbreak.

Guilt is generally associated with the feeling a person has when he or she has done something society deems bad or evil.

Let's detail the relationship between various components to the guilt cycle:
Too much force/action/motion = violence, crime, wrongdoing.
Insufficient force/action/motion = negligence, crime, wrongdoing.
Violence, negligence, crime, wrongdoing = weakened survival for the victim, strengthened survival for the perpetrator.

The length of time a victim experiences the pain can be a measure of the damage caused by the abuse. But it is dependent purely on the state of mind and attitude of the victim. Time can allow the victim a personal rebuilding to the point of overcoming the effects of the damage. Ultimately, the victim can potentially benefit from the experience if ample healing has occurred.

Guilt is an emotional and mental state of the victim, where the victim also sees self as the perpetrator of or at least as a contributor to the deed or crime. (No; it's not a mistake: the victim can also be associated to the victimizing crime!)

On a social level, actions are declared wrong deeds or crimes by legislation, based on the predominant social perception of the severity of the damage caused the victim. A society is generally incapable of accurately assessing or establishing the degree of damage to the victim's abstract characteristics, such as pain. Therefore, an arbitrary, somewhat educated estimate of money value is assigned, based on tradition and circumstances. The nature of the damage includes, but is not exclusive to, the emotional, creative, motivational, cognitive and intellectual facets of a person.

A person generates guilt with his conviction of having committed a crime. This often happens with crimes wherein his or society's attitude contains a subtle assumption that the victim is responsible. Rape is the classical crime wherein the attitude of guilt of the victim is painfully present. If one is a victim of abuse, he is also a participant, and almost invariably there is the intimation that the victim in some way contributed, provoked, or in some way brought it upon himself by his own actions. Guilt is the feeling and understanding that the transgression (the victim's belief that somehow he or she did something to cause it, thereby becoming an accessory to the crime) shouldn't have occurred, and is often accompanied by a continuous feeling of regret and a need to stop the action from taking place.

It is immediately apparent that much of the evaluation of the damage done to the victim is purely subjective and personal. Much depends on the opinion or feelings of the person making the evaluation.

Guilt and Violence

A few years ago I was walking a commercial street of a large city at dusk, and was about to get into my automobile after having deposited a briefcase in the back seat. By the time I closed the rear door, I found myself flanked by two youths that spoke to me in words I scarcely understood. While I was mentally attempting to discover what they wanted, they, without waiting for a response, began to physically assault me. One of them grabbed the right sleeve of my coat with his right hand, while attempting to put his hands in my pocket. The other struck my face with his right hand, while in my left flank I felt the blow of his fist which was holding an object that made his hand a more powerful weapon.

I was so surprised at the moment of the attack that I was experiencing outrage. At the same time, I also experienced the terror that I believed was emanating from the youths themselves. During the struggle I attempted to ward the hand of the assailant on the right from reaching into the pockets of my garments, and on the left, trying to shield against the striking fist on my face. A moment later I was down on one knee, surprised by the effect of the thrust of a fist square into my left cheek. I continued to struggle. While on the ground, anticipating the high possibility of becoming unconscious by the next blow of a fist, I maneuvered my body toward a metal gate of a warehouse. With my body and feet, I began to strike the gate. This alerted people inside, who came out in time, startling the youths enough to cause them to flee.

Oddly, when my friends came out from inside and I saw them looking at me, I was filled with embarrassment. The physical wounds did not last more than one or two weeks, but the embarrassment and some elements of guilt were there much longer.

Now I had my guilt to study. As time passed, I came to understand more clearly the ideas that go through the victim's mind during and after an event of violence.

I was a winner in this event (that is, I escaped with my life, as well as prevented them from carrying out what I believe was a theft). Yet I couldn't help but feel I was wrong in some way. Somehow I felt wrong for having placed myself at such risk.

*I was guilty of stupidity for not having seen the youths in advance, therefore making it impossible to prevent the attack in the first place.

*I failed to adequately defend myself and was not able to punish the assailants.

*I was not the winner; I was the victim.

At the police station the next day, I was made to wait for over an hour (the police had failed to arrive the day before, when called at the time of the event). During the wait, and then throughout the interview, while a report was being prepared, I sensed that the police where uncertain as to whether I was assaulted or whether I had actually become involved in a brawl.

The lady friend who was with me at the time did not hesitate to exclaim: "How could you be so careless!"

This is socially assigned guilt. Sometimes we, as victims, find ourselves feeling guilty of stupidity for allowing an offence to occur and not having the foresight to see it coming in time to prevent it, among other things.

Guilt and Abuse

Keep in mind the definitions of violence and abuse, so that you are able to maintain your own sense of judgment to apply to yourself as you see appropriate.

I taught a group of young people some years ago. As part of the curriculum, I would elicit topics of discussion for the practice of public speaking and effective use of the language.

Chapter Fifteen — Violence and Abuse

Sexual abuse was one such topic. The students were required to make a class presentation. A young woman of 23 presented her essay. Between tears and emotional stalls, she related her personal experience of abuse at the hands of a beloved uncle. Since she was the last person to speak before the break, there was time for only a few minutes of discussion. The outrage in the whole class was visible, and most of the students were moved and emotionally vocal. The guilt she felt associated with the abuse was mentioned, though not really explained. She was the victim, yet she was suffering guilt from the event.

The young woman remained behind while the rest of the students went on break. She sat as if to rest, but her attention focused on me. I looked at her and asked her, "Something you didn't mention in your essay you want to talk to me about?"

Without a word she started crying and continued crying for nearly 15 minutes. Finally she spoke. "I enjoyed it all throughout the time it was happening." She continued crying, and I placed my hand on her shoulder without speaking. She spoke again, "I turned him in to the police." At this point she cried even harder and almost uncontrollably.

Finally she said, "I loved him, and I still love him, and I betrayed him."

I had no real idea how to deal with this, beyond the point of attempting to quietly comfort her. I said, "I understand; it seems you feel guilty for having turned in a person you loved… And for having enjoyed something you think you shouldn't have enjoyed…" She nodded, assenting. My comment seemed to have calmed her down, and she rose to go freshen up.

This young woman was guilty of enjoying an activity that she understood society detested. By enjoying it, she was in essence contributing to the crime. This was a terrible secret to carry. She also had to betray someone she loved. This is a serious violation of one's personal integrity, as she saw it.

Often, the recognition of having been involved in something bad, or that which is deemed as bad by society, takes place at or toward the end of the actual act. We are assailed by fear and embarrassment. "What will they say when they find out? They'll know I did this!" Our learned ideas begin to distort what actually took place. Ultimately, a person is not able to rationalize the event at all, because what she has experienced is inherently wrong in the eyes of society. She keeps locked very deep inside her the idea that she might have enjoyed some aspects of the act. In her mind there is no one who could possibly treat her with any kindness or respect, knowing she may actually have enjoyed such a vile act. The door to any understanding of the event is slammed shut from the moment she feels an ounce of pleasure.

Guilt finds its way into the very core of a woman or a man who has experienced such an event. It grows like a cancer, often for a lifetime. Looking at the event for what it was in the moment, and understanding why it was enjoyable on some level, is paramount to the resolution of guilt and the ultimate happiness of the person involved.

Guilt and Life-Summary

A child is born with a completely clean slate. Realities build within his consciousness through repetitive exposure to experiences. The child's basic perceptions are of love and fear, and his early reality is formed based on these two perceptions. Guilt can be impressed upon the child by loving parents as much as through violence or abuse by others.

Those for whom the child develops stronger bonds of love are the strongest influences in building that child's sense of good and evil, right and wrong. None exists before that. The basis for a child's reality is shaped by the child's perception of the actions done by a loved one. If the loved one withdraws love from something or someone, the child sees the something or someone as bad.

Before the cycle of guilt is imprinted, the child has no sense of either good or evil. Any intimate contact with a loved one is normally a source of pleasure to the child, since the

Chapter Fifteen — Violence and Abuse

child thrives on being the focus of a loved one.

It may be unfathomable to think that pleasure is present when there is outright physical damage to the body, or extreme emotional duress such as rape under imminent threat of physical damage. However, invariably actions preceding the pain are perceived as pleasurable experiences, yet, obscured by the subsequent pain.

Another source of guilt involves the types of acts by a child which are perceived as transgressions by the loving adults, in an environment where there is no visible violence. Usually these transgressions are acts against the will of a parent. For the child, Going against a parent contains the pleasure of standing up to, even a loved one. What usually follows the child's act is a series of communications (sometimes even in the form of silence) from the loved one to the child that impress upon the child a conviction of his badness in connection to the action. The child begins to feel wicked. This produces guilt and remorse. There is a mental effort on the part of the child to keep the event from happening again, and generally, later in life, an insistent denial that the abuse happened at all. This is the source of the inability to make decisions that many experience through life. These individuals are emotionally poised to be wrong, so the tendency is indecision, rather than risk being confronted with the disapproving eyes of others.

It is a common belief that guilt is solely induced internally by the person's conscience, but, as you can see from the above description of the guilt process, the person's internal mental activity that accepts or promotes guilt is a reaction to the external influence of people perceived as more powerful. What parents, respected associates, or loved ones have communicated to a person will have prompted the guilt; it transmits a conviction that one has done something wrong.

The child's understanding there is no entitlement to experience pleasure from the event, further reinforced guilt. This one factor makes the guilt build upon itself, making it many-fold stronger. Because the child experiences some degree of pleasure preceding the event for which they later will feel guilt, the child eventually comes to own personal responsibility, if not the outright personal causation of the event.

The ultimate reaction of the individual takes one of two possible roads: The first is to shut down completely and avoid experiences perceived as related with the subject matter touched by the abuse. (For example, a child convinced of little intelligence, will avoid experiences perceived to exceed that intelligence, such as a complex table game, and will do so as an adult.) This manifests in indecisiveness and inaction throughout most of life. The second is to rebel against the oppressive force that causes continuous guilt. This is followed by an internal declaration of independence, and the assertion that the acts that prompt the guilt were not truly wrong actions. In order to assert that declaration, the person will perpetrate the same violations upon others as a method of asserting rightness, and as a way of reclaiming the power lost in the original event.

Guilt acquired because of violations of one's personal rules or private code of honor such as errors, mistakes and omissions that do not normally constitute violations imposed upon a person, surrenders easily to self-forgiveness.

On the other hand, the guilt that arises from the breach of a social code is much more difficult to eradicate, since the violation is rarely ever forgiven by society. One who has served time in prison is rarely able erase the mark and is subject to continued punishment by way of exclusion from complete social acceptance. The effect can be just as devastating when the transgression involves two individuals in a relationship. A lover's condemnation can make the real or imagined transgression just as unforgivable. The lover will give up his/her life, living in fear and bondage of guilt in an attempt to repair the wrongdoing.

The victim of abuse is harmed to a greater degree than the perpetrator. The latter has greater personal control over his actions, than the victim. The person enforcing the guilt or perpetrating violence or abuse carried out a somewhat premeditated action within his control; it was an act of will. The victim did not perceive herself as in control over the rule he broke (especially unwritten rules) or the violence he received. The victim is now using the guilt in an attempt to control the event after the fact, by an emotional effort to have the event not have happened. This guilt is an effort by the victim to convince self that the event never took place. The victim is continuously attempting to prevent herself from carrying out the transgression.

    The specific methods of healing these wounds require more time and attention to detail. The only effective permanent cure, if you will, is to heal the wounds of abuse the parents have undergone, early enough to give them the clarity needed to avoid repeating the pattern with their own offspring. Additionally more practical research is needed in order to refine the healing procedures or discover new ones.

You are now at a point when the connection is more stable. You have ironed out all details of agreements, practices, intentions, desires, and realities. You have even argued, fought, and resolved differences. Now it's time to take the relationship to the next level.

Part V
Nurturing

Being deeply loved by someone gives you strength,
While loving someone deeply gives you courage.
~ Lao Tzu ~

Chapter Sixteen
The Magic Key

Yes. If there is anything that will sweep another being reeling with pleasure and delight, and will convert any emotion into pure joy, that one thing is unconditional love.

Unconditional love is not blind. It is not the overlooking of unpleasant or dangerous things, nor is it a pretense that all is well and beautiful and wonderful everywhere. Humans live in very challenging environments in stressful social, economic, and political conditions. The character of humans is such that we are capable of perpetrating the most unthinkable cruelties. In this backdrop, unconditional love is all but impossible.

Yet, there is a road, and it is, albeit rocky, still travel worthy. The trek can indeed be made. The road can indeed be traveled.

We discussed some of the mechanics of love earlier, and spoke of harmonic resonance and awareness of connection. These things are the seeds of unconditional love. In fact, the first instant of a connection is likely to be unconditional love. It begins to deteriorate the moment one views the rational practicalities of life on planet earth, when one begins to think about how the connection should manifest in the physical environment, and reservations about physical survival begins to frighten lovers.

Love continues to break down when codes of conduct, whether accepted or not, are enforced and broken. Each expects that his or her code of conduct will be followed, even though often the other never saw nor understood what was expected at the beginning, when love was unconditional. These are the expectations each assumes the other has already subscribed to. Love continues to deteriorate each time the lovers interpret evil and deceit in the behavior of the other. You think he is lying to you and cheating on you, even before you had any agreements where mutually acceptable behavior was ever discussed or agreed upon. And it crumbles when he in fact has been devious and has been lying, and deceitful, pretending a love he no longer feels.

It deteriorates while you are attempting to shape the relationship into a safe haven, which you will attempt to secure with demands, and other pressures and prescriptions.
How can you ensure a loving connection will be nourished and last? Following are the impossible acts of love. I don't know any human person who is capable of such complete love. A great deal of experience, however, tells me that the closer you come to it, the greater the joy. You might like to try these actions as best as you can, with the intention of going as high as you can, thus improve your love daily. It's worth a serious look.

When you DO these acts of love, you love; that is love; the more thorough you do them, the deeper in love do you fall!

First Act of Love

Love unconditionally. Unconditional love is not developed and is not manufactured. It is not something built at will, but it can be. It is that which occurs at the very first instant the individuals become aware of a connection, which is beyond a purely social politeness. It is what has been called love at first sight. Love at first sight has received a bad reputation, and dismissed as infatuation, the bewitching of uncontrollable irrational attraction. It has been dubbed irrational, impractical, a waste of time, a deception, a delusion, a fantasy. We can more accurately say, love at the first moment of recognition. Yes. It can appear irrational, and it is fantastical, and often impractical. But above all, it is the core of creation. It is the source of life; it is the force that turned yesterday's fantasies into today's realities, yesterday's impracticalities into today's efficiencies, yesterday's irrationalities into today's wisdom, yesterday's delusions into today's illusions, and tomorrow's realities. It is neither a waste of time nor a deception. It is the mishandling that love endures in the social environment has made it unpalatable, and often unattainable.

Love is the merging and bonding and the expanding of bonds into new lives, and the transformation of creations into ever-greater creations.

Second Act of Love

Allow, Accept, and Embrace Unconditionally. A child looks up to the parent, and he doesn't care about the appearance, and the behavior, and any of the parent's characteristics. Nothing moves one more than to have bestowed total acceptance upon all of one's characteristics. This is not mere tolerance of things you find unacceptable. This is unconditional acceptance of all that the other person is. It is also the ability to understand the other person's rightness and validity of the reasons for their existence, and their joy for what they are or how they are at any given moment. It is joining them in their joy, by finding out who the other is, and seeing this not as simply acceptable, but admirable. It is joining the other person in their activities and cooperating with great joy. It means a deep understanding of the things in their heart and in their life and in their mind. It is a deep understanding of their underlying rightness. It implies the ability to receive whatever the other person gives. Beyond that is a higher level of allowance or acceptance:

Embrace unconditionally. Embracing unconditionally suggests something beyond the mere passive concept of accepting. In accepting, one simply allows something to be.

When you embrace you actively participate and creatively contribute, and rejoice in the life and the acts of the one you love.

Embracing sees love as a wisp of scented air sitting on the open palm; if the fist is closed into a grip, it slips through the fingers, and it's gone.
Is it simple enough?

Yes, it is a nearly impossible task.

Third Act Love

Give unconditionally. This is as simple as it sounds. The more you give, the greater your own satisfaction. We are not talking about physical gifts. At the top of the list is to give your complete honesty, yourself in all its facets, your attention in abundance. It means to give your openness, and your life, your past, your future, and your dreams. To give is to do things from within your heart to enhance your loved one's life. The giving can be unlimited. Give yourself, openly and honestly.

In giving there is also the willingness to receive. When you experience the joys of complete giving, you also give the loved ones the opportunity to give to you, so they too will experience the joys of giving.

Love is the creative force of the universe, and the substance upon which all universes exist; it is an infinite pool from which anyone can drink. Love emanates in all directions from within. One or more persons can connect to it, and some degree of co-generative power develops between them which enhances and gives the joy of the awareness of the interchanges of these flows of energy between them.

Love isn't something you have for someone; it isn't all sweetness and light. It isn't pretending all is beautiful and all is love, while blind to the homeless and the outcast's sorrows. Love is the courage to cross the fires of hell, and reconstruct the self as the phoenix from the ashes. It is having the courage to know what one sees, and the integrity to act upon it. As Levine best expressed it, "Love is the only rational act."

Chapter Sixteen — The Magic Key

Test The Magic Key-Quick Test

All right, you just don't want to wait to do all the things in the book. You want a quick way of getting at least a taste of how to feel love. Here is a little exercise that will give you a sense of what I'm talking about.

* Go to a fairly crowded place where people are likely to stay within sight for long periods of time, like a park, or a sport event, a restaurant.

* Choose someone, anyone, at random, and focus on them comfortably and get the feeling of (a) being aware of a connection, (b) allowing completely; totally embracing whatever is in front of you about that person; and (c) giving completely.

Getting the feeling of something means to actually feel or sense in the body and the mind what it might be like to experience the reality of what someone is contemplating. To see this process work, you have to persuade yourself or imagine it is really happening. Imagine that there is a connection and that you are aware of it; you are completely allowing the person to be totally as they are (as you perceive them); and that you are committed to give them totally of yourself and all that is you.

This type of pretend is very useful in imagining experiences and creating mental simulations to flex the emotions, and loosen locked up, or otherwise inactive feelings and emotions. Be careful! They can become quite real.
Would it be too far fetched to say, "To find love, choose someone to love, and then love them."

My Heart and How They Won It

The acts of love that comprise the magic key are neatly packaged and might, at times, be much too difficult to follow. Everyone is able to do the acts of love to some extent already. Let me show you in a more visible and practical dimension that will illustrate them further from the receiving end of love.

My own experiences are not unlike what you have felt and what others feel. In my own experience the first impact I sensed that has caught my attention is when someone has a genuine admiration for the person that I am. This is the embracing aspect of love. This is produces the sense of connection and harmonic resonance.

The second impact that I sensed was a clear indication that they were actually touched or moved by what they perceived in me. This admiration is not a mere praise to patronize or simply be polite. This admiration touches one very deeply. It's unmistakable. It's also the aspect of allowance, and acceptance, which manifests as compassion and understanding.
The third impact was that of genuine, honest, expressions of embracing. It is not only, "Yes, I really understand where you are coming from." It is "Wow I can see why you would want such thing. I find that attractive as well." It is the embracing of those very private realities that you think no one would understand or like about you, and they might even think less of you if they knew it.

When the ugly you, is totally embraced, you know and feel you've been touched with a great love. The task of lovingly embracing the unacceptable is truly the iron that cast the crucible of undying love, a rare experience indeed. It isn't something that simply amuses or catches your attention. It is something that strikes deeply and permanently. When you are the one who has embraced what were once seen as another's monsters, you will know you have conquered love.

Such impacts may tend to occur almost simultaneously, and avalanche into a powerful connection where those involved are sure the other was the power behind the connection. "I couldn't have felt this way without you." "What has happened is that you brought the best out of me." "You had the courage to bring us here." Sounds like the first love?

Chapter Sixteen — The Magic Key

The person who tries to live alone will not succeed as a human being. His heart withers if it does not answer another heart. His mind shrinks away if he hears only the echoes of his own thoughts and finds no other inspiration.
~ Pearl S. Buck ~

Chapter Seventeen
Woman-Mother

There is no activity of greater importance in the entire universe than the act of creation. All stems from it, all grows because of it, all lives as a result of it. Within human activities that act is contained in the creative and nurturing power of woman, in a measure above all other creative human characteristics.

People in the 20th and 21st century societies have been through or are coming through a period when there is a pervasive sense of contempt and disrespect for the function of a mother. She's supposed to go to work outside the home, and leave her children to be cared for by strangers at an even higher cost, and higher risk of failure to deliver that very nurturing upon which the society depends to turn out productive, contributing individuals. When she does not go outside the home to work, she is more often than not in a state of poverty.

Should the society care about such conditions? Many say, "Why should anyone receive free money from the society (through the state)?" One who would ask that question is showing a lack of understanding of basic economic realities. Without putting you through a course on basic economics and the elements affecting the distribution of production, let me ask you one simple question:

Were pregnant mothers dropped off from some other society into our society? Were they foisted on us by an enemy nation or from outside the planet? On a broader scale:

Were the poor and the indigent that walk the streets without food or attention abandoned in our streets by some unknown evil? Were the prisoners and criminals in our jails unloaded upon our society by unknown entities or unknown forces?

What these three types of social conditions have in common is that all of them are the products of and part of the society. The individual in that condition is 100% responsible for being in that condition. The society is also 100% responsible.

But until the society can be re-educated by you, the Mother, you can expect things to go on as usual. Woe the society who fails to support its core of love and life.

Ultimate Power-Ultimate Weapon

Nothing can lift a man so high, give him so much confidence, provide him with a great deal of pride, and be an endless pool of inspiration as can the love of a woman. Nothing can bring a man so low, remove his self-esteem, deprive him his pride, and emasculate him as the withdrawal of that love. For the moment it is irrelevant to explain or analyze the reasons for that. Superficial inspection suggests that the styles of differences in raising men and raising women may account for it. The role that had been defined for women did not restrict a woman's emotional development. Consequently, I contemplate that she has a greater ability and capacity for love than man, while not absolutely, at least in a general way. Having said that, one would have to wonder why the problems involving social position for women begin with a relationship with a man at any stage.

The power to love, and the power to withdraw love are two powerful tools that woman can employ to maintain a balance of power and some semblance of justice.

The ancient Sabine people were overtaken by conquest by their enemy. The Sabine women confronted and persuaded the enemy that before continuing to sack the city, they allow women to leave with whatever they could carry. The women walked out of the city carrying their men upon their shoulders. The enemy leader was emotionally disarmed at the sight and evidence of such profound love.

Consider finally reasons why women have not employed such tools as effectively as they might have been employed. I attribute it to her willingness to sacrifice, and willingness to allow humiliation and suffering while her vulnerability is at its highest; when the protection and nurturing of her children are paramount in her life.

Ultimate Responsibility

With power comes the responsibility to use it, and how to use it.

Women are behind every social scene; you are the wives and lovers of the men you allow to make the laws and run the social institutions. You have been taught to stand behind your man. Stand beside him when his direction and integrity are just and rational. But stand in front of him, stop him, and redirect him when his judgment is clouded, and you see him prepared to perpetrate cruelties or abuses upon others. If you allow him to move through, be prepared to watch your own powers as nurturer diminish. In relinquishing this responsibility, you will see the disappearance of your powers as the educator of the young into honest, powerful, and free human beings, each with a profound sense of integrity.

Women, you are the mothers, the friends, the wives, and the lovers of those men that are capable of doing whatever you will allow them. Start training him today. Stand by his side, not behind him, and when you have to, stand in front of him, and don't permit him to be unjust or dishonest. If you do, you will age ever so much faster, and your brow will show the burden you allowed him to create for others.

If you allow him to do thing for which you will lose respect for him, then when you lose your respect for him, you will also have lost him.

Mother Feminist

There are men and women are in the society, trying to gain equal recognition, respect, and other rights for women. This is as it should be.

There is an important area where the focus seems to have been lost. In the life of every woman there are one or more men over whom they have a great deal of influence: husbands, sons, fiancés and friends. One of the best ways women can achieve their objective along women's rights, is by educating their young, and the men in their lives.

This does become difficult when the society is doing everything it can to separate the children from the mother as early as it can, and send them to a faceless daycare facility, where if it's not regulated by state law, it's certainly regulated by the personal beliefs and ideas of the owners! Then, the society educates the children, not just the females, but also the males, according to the status quo; thereby neither gains the proper perspective on the matter of equality.

Should I advise women to play a stronger role as mother in educating their young, instead of sending them off to the care of others? Can this advice be carried out in the presence of dubious education which promotes the contrary? I'm not asserting that woman belongs in the home; I'm merely declaring that social pressures should not force her out of it.

The woman's choice: self-sufficient freedom or the homemaker who must rely on her ability to demand from the mate (or society—which, we discussed, is reluctant to provide). I believe both can be achieved. And what's more important, woman should be supported in such endeavors, as such is a natural right. The child-bearing years and offspring-rearing years are not the entire life of a woman, and rationally shared with the mate, life can be a full and rewarding for both, provided it's based on a sound contract which considers the rights and responsibilities of both.

Commitment

Once the emotional elements of the connection are well cemented, and you know that there is love that will maintain the connection, you are now ready. You can now consider commitment.

Commitment is an interesting word. Its root implies so many things that are also generally understood as being part of the meaning of the word. It is the act of committing. To commit, comes from Latin Com + mittere. Com = with, together, joint, jointly. Mittere = to send, put, place.
(Literally: send together, put or place together.) To put into charge or trust, to obligate or pledge oneself.

In common usage to say "I make a commitment to you," or "I commit myself to you," means, I put my full trust in you; I obligate myself to you that you may trust me to do as I have said I will do.

That further translates into the specific promises people make to one another, whether it is a business commitment, a commitment in a relationship, or a commitment to the accomplishment of a task.

Commitment can be explicit with very specific promises, or tacit with small areas where trust and promise develop and are implied in the actions taken by the individuals involved.

We have been educated to think and believe that we never give our word unless we are completely sure that we can do what we say we will do. Also once we give your word, it is more important to carry it out, even to the expense of our lives. That is not the real practice in most modern societies.

Ask any number of people, and the prevalent response is, "Don't trust anyone." In this atmosphere it's nearly impossible to make or trust a commitment. Nevertheless, be one to still believe in your own word, and be willing to carry it out, and do so, no matter what the personal cost. In so doing, you will restore the hope that the trust in one's word is sacred.

Do you need to protect yourself from others, since deceit is so prevalent? It is better to trust people, take them at their word, and insist they honor it. Trust until you are given reasons to do otherwise, and insist on reparation when trust is broken. By trusting people as a general rule, you set the stage where potential betrayals will show themselves early enough that any loss will be very small. It seems that there is a discernable pattern here. When you trust someone, your trust is visible. If another has a propensity to abuse that trust, they will abuse it within a short time. They will betray that trust in small but visible ways from the beginning. This should be your signal that if someone cannot be trusted in small matters, they certainly cannot be trusted with carrying out a lifetime commitment. Such persons can be trained to become trustworthy, but it's a hard chore to undertake, with an unpredictable training curve.

Beyond these basic ideas, you have your experience and your observations to draw upon in making accurate judgments as to whom and to what degree you can trust. But do not make the mistake of generalizing past failures in trust by attributing a quality of mistrust to a category of people, whether it be in reference to gender (men/women can not be trusted), race, (this or that race of people cannot be trusted), or any other group.

Finally, once you have brought a connection to the personal commitment that is mutually agreed, you can now establish how the connection will appear to others, in the social arena.

Chapter Seventeen

Woman-Mother

Love has no desire but to fulfill itself. To melt and be like a running brook that sings its melody to the night. To wake at dawn with a winged heart and give thanks for another day of loving.

~Kahlil Gibran~

Chapter Eighteen
The Social Side of a Connection

Once the emotional elements of the connection are well cemented, and you know that there is love to sustain it, you are ready to iron out how the connection will survive the social environment, and what shall be the nature of the connection.

The sexual roles and the games played at this stage are key elements in the relationship of men and women in the society at large. None would care to acknowledge this, but the roles established at an early stage are replayed throughout life, and are reflected in the professional, religious, social, and political arenas.

The stance you develop here will affect you in your future, your career, and your life in the society. There is an incredibly tenuous balance to be maintained here in the sexual roles. They tend to extend beyond the bedroom and into the clubroom, the dance room, and the proverbial boardroom. It becomes your personal responsibility to maintain yourself above the stereotype you are cast into by your surroundings, be it schoolmates, social systems or parental training. I'll say this in passing now: Your behavior as a woman at this stage is what will either change the balance of powers or perpetuate the glass ceiling women find in the current social setting.

Pregnancy & Other Sexual Fall Out

If you have not already established your personal standards about sexual behavior, it's time that you do so now.

There are some serious matters you have to consider, and have solutions already worked out and agreed before hand, because thinking about solutions when the problem is imminent will almost invariably result in regrettable solutions.

Pregnancy is one such matter. Yes. If there is a possibility of pregnancy, you are not in the percentage of women to which this will not happen. So, don't operate on that assumption that it will not happen to you, unless you have taken the type of precautions that eliminate that possibility.

Whether you think you are otherwise safe, if the possibility of pregnancy is there, and you welcome it, you have to be ready to deal with it and all that comes from it. If you're in the bottom 70% of income ladder, chances is that a child will add significant burdens to your relationship, not to mention the burden to your family and friends.

Options & Safety Nets

A pregnancy will directly affect at least one third of your life, and indirectly all of it. If you become pregnant at a very early age unbeknownst to a possibly departed boyfriend, you have the option of remaining silent, and raising the child by yourself. Children are born to all layers of society, rich poor and in between. The lower down the income ladder you are in, the greater the burden. If your parents have already become aware of the child, and are accustomed to the idea, and will accept the child into the family, you have a fair chance. If you are in your midlife having already experienced such trials, you are in a better position to give advice than I am.

As a mother, you may never see the child as a burden, since to you the child is probably the product of your love. A mother will often undergo unbelievable sacrifices for her children, including tolerating injustices, inhumanities, and cruelty. How frequent do single mothers find themselves without necessary support?

Whether you are at the beginning of unsupported motherhood, or have already lived through it, you must awaken your personal power. If you don't, you will continue to be too vulnerable to fight, and you will also become too willing to accept vilification, humiliation, and abuses.

When I started taking a close look at what I perceived as built-in disrespect and off-handed disregard for women, the incidents of unsupported motherhood became sorely visible as more prevalent than I had previously imagined. In addition to the lack of social support, I became aware that this group of women is generally more susceptible to other unpleasant circumstances because of their inherent vulnerability, and in their vulnerability they endure this unpleasantness to avoid risk potential risk to their children.

What I witnessed in every case were shabby and unresolved situations, and women who lived in quiet contentment that the injustices they underwent were a worthwhile price to protect their children from the cruelty of men who instituted the social structures that permit them to perpetrate such abuses.

Our social structure doesn't seem to appreciate a woman's valuable contribution to the social fabric. It is clear that a woman is by biological design in the most advantageous position to carry and raise children! If she ends up alone or if she chooses to raise her child alone she receives no help, except at poverty standards of social welfare. She is even thought of as lazy or incompetent for staying at home and taking care of children.

This is a blindness our society will pay for dearly. As a young woman, you find yourself in a position that requires you to start building your safety nets early on. As much as you may want to ignore it, you are wise to start the planning of your future.

Your parents, who have consented to accept the child into the family, however, might insist that you get state help because your income alone will not take care of the child. But, you've been indoctrinated to believe that no one should really get something for nothing, therefore, why should anyone even you, go on the dole?

When you finally consent because you hardly have a choice, you are going to be subjected to the most excruciating, humiliating investigations and questioning. You leave the welfare offices feeling not only humiliated for having had a child, but as guilty of giving birth as you would be for having taken a life. This is one of those little injustices a vulnerable new mother will allow herself to be subjected to, for the sake of her children. You who have endured these things know much better than I do. If you wish to see first hand how the system works, go on any early morning before sun-up, and talk to some of the people who stand on welfare lines.

A social Contract vs. A Contract of Love

The sexual/marital agreement is an option rarely exercised by women. As we discussed earlier, parents gave women away to their daughter's future mate with a handshake and assurances from the new owner that he'd take care of her. Marriage controls, like population counts, became a political necessity of political powers, kings and despots. The first sex license was thus born: Marriage. Sex without a license was known as adultery or fornication. You understand this is a raw way of looking at the matter of social contracts of sexual relationships. (Christian historical accounts attribute to the advent of clerical and later civil laws in the early centuries to the continuous demand upon prelates to arbitrate in marital disputes in an environment where no written law had existed. Whatever the real reasons may be, they are of little value to address modern problems.)

I bring it up in this manner, so you realize that the sexual/marriage contract may need to be treated as a social contract as well as a private contract between individuals. You and your partner might feel that you would never abuse each other or violate what is agreed upon. Nevertheless, many things have to be agreed upon in order to avoid potential disagreements which eventually court disaster. Issues such as unwanted pregnancy, abortion and rights to parenthood have to be known, understood and agreed upon. Review your own ideas concerning your personal rights to the state of your body and your health. You must unequivocally claim your right of determination over your person, which has precedence over any other.

If you wish to consider this from a purely moral or religious position, such decisions remain your exclusive domain, except as otherwise agreed upon with your partner. Have humans been granted the right to regulate or judge the moral or religious conduct of their fellow humans? Claims to that effect are difficult to substantiate beyond the obvious need to prevent harm to others, aspects of which can often be subjective. You will have to live with whatever you do. Therefore, you have to know what you are going to do, and an agreement to the effect must exist. If an agreement cannot be reached, it's a good reason not to continue taking risks. It is easier for you to deal with issues while it's not a pressing problem, than when it accidentally becomes a major disaster.

One final point to consider if you ultimately choose to bear a child without the support of the sperm donoran intentional distinction from fatheris a simple fact that a child, not born out of mutual consent, is the mother's child. It is the mother's choice if and who the child's father should be, with the consent of the father to be. The sperm donor is not the father. The father is a parent who has accepted the mother's invitation to be the father, whether this person is the sperm donor or not.

In this connection, you must also ensure you build a support network of responsible family members. Remember, society has lost its willingness to take responsibility to help its members in this arena. One wonders about the purposes for which social structures and governments were created, if not to ensure the survival and moderate comfort of its members.

Ramifications of the Marriage Contract

While I may be vociferously opposing the social order, I am indeed a member of it, because most of our lives take place within a social context. A lifetime agreement or any form of association falls within a social context, therefore such agreements should contain some semblance of a socially acceptable format, whether it is a standard license or a written and witnessed document. Otherwise you have no social support for any position and you cannot claim any protection or rights that the society vests on such associations. Verbal agreements are often acceptable, but their existence is difficult to prove, since the proof is based on actions consistently executed over time that suggest an agreement existed. Often, this is not the case.

Marriage is essentially a legal contract. You must carefully review the potential problems, not only in the execution of the contract, but also in the event of termination of the contract. The points that follow are based on the major concerns expressed in interviews with women from different social layers, and from careful observation throughout the years.

Marriage (or a lifetime agreement) should be treated as if it were a legal contract. Anyone entering into it should be thoroughly prepared for any legal ramifications of such a contract. You must be aware of the prevailing laws in the region where you live. Where the laws of the land are deficient or unfairly weighed, the parties should do whatever necessary to adjust any inequities written into laws issued by legislatures and government, and modify the effects of those laws by whatever legal means available, including prenuptial agreements. In some localities the law can override private contracts. If the locale wherein you expect to marry does not allow private contracts to override the state laws, then you would be well advised to enter into some other type of association, instead of a traditional marriage, the private agreements of which are enforceable by law.

Sometimes there is a carelessness in entering such contract on the part of both parties based on the false security of, "We love each other; I trust him implicitly. She'll never do anything to harm me." I've spoken to hundreds of women who made that very statement to themselves years earlier, to eventually find themselves in intolerable difficulties.

A social contract dealing with exchanges between people, such as the mechanics of living together and producing offspring, has little if anything to do with the emotional elements of the relationship or connection. Dealing with both elements as if they were only emotional matters, has always and invariably caused interminable problems. One of the principle ingredients to a workable contract is when all details of the contract are well known and understood, and agreed upon. The volume of undesirable results from behavior that dismisses functional issues as emotional ones, speaks eloquently in favor of understanding all aspects of a contract before committing to it.

The word marriage has such mystical and romantic connotations, and carries such a powerful image of undying love and passion. It carries the illusion of the materialization of all dreams. It implies the commitment of an undying loyalty. It suggests the total forgiveness of all past sins and a very high tolerance of all misdeeds yet to be done. It is packed with all the wishes that upon a star once were made. It is filled with a never-ending state of bliss; it is the happily-ever-after from the Fairy Tale phase. The word that encompasses all of those things may yet to been coined; perhaps it has been called unconditional love; but not necessarily marriage.

While love demands little or nothing in its purest form, living in a social environment does. Therefore, with the utmost love in your heart, and with the care and responsibility to ensure the safety and durability of that love, choose a structure that will sustain the connection. When you choose marriage upon which to build a kind of life that materializes your dreams, and as means to secure your social interests, you are immediately taking your unconditional love and placing it in the realm of a socio-political contract, which has its prescribed condition every step of the way. The marriage contract does not guarantee love will prevail.

Entering into a marriage in an attempt to secure unconditional love is a declaration of your doubt of that very love. A solemn statement of love does not require anyone's approval or license. It can be made at will. It does not require publicity or a public declaration to gain validity.

Adding a dimension of sacredness to unconditional love by means of a public declaration of vows in front of your congregation carries the warmth of those of like minds, and the stimulation of warm feelings of joining with others in unity of thought. But the private declarations, sworn on your life and on your honor will be filled with like sacredness. Without this private declaration, the public one is but an empty vessel. Once the private declarations and sacredness is in place, go ahead and place that into the social context by putting the agreement in writing. Had the judge who enjoined them with the spoken vows, till death do us part also given them a document of the vows to sign, I assure you, the act of signing alone would cause many to think on its violation with greater care.

Follow your personal beliefs and preferences and the ideas you find acceptable. Are there alternate symbolic ceremonies of love that can add a dimension of sacredness to the union, which can be performed in front of one's kin and friends, beyond the traditional? Many people create their own sacred ritual. It is important that the society evolve new ceremonies which create indelible bonds, since the traditional marriage ceremonies seem to leave open too many easy exits.

One aspect of marriage is a socio-political contract. The other is its symbolic representation of vows of Love. Approach each accordingly.

Contract Issues to Consider

In addition to those suggested so far in a generalized way, here are some of the things many women advise taking into consideration before actually entering into the socio-legal side of a marriage contract:

* Disposition/distribution of the property in the event of termination should be agreed beforehand.

* It is not advisable to change names, and assume the family name of the male. Many advise combining last names into new compound names.

* Assets either individual brings into the relationship remain theirs.

* Is it not advisable to immediately pool properties or assets brought into the association to the exclusion of personal control over personal assets; this includes cash accounts, savings or checking. When this becomes a preferable convenience it obviously requires a sense of unquestionable trust. Most women I've spoken to recommend keeping your identity, and maintaining control over your personal resources and property, such as vehicles and homes.

* Methods of running the operating budget of the association must be known, understood, and agreed before hand.

* As for property acquired during the time of the association, it has been suggested that, because in many places the law considers those acquisitions to be common property which must be divided upon termination of the association, objects of value that are purchased during the association should have separate documentation. Meaning, a determination should be made at the time of purchase as to who shall take possession of the given purchases, in the event of termination. When no such agreements have been made, in most cases I believe the woman should have the final word on most household items. This opinion is based on the assumption that the woman is likely to be confronted with more difficulties after dissolution.

* Disposition of assets upon the death of one of the parties should also be taken into account.

* Plan the entire course of the association in terms of: a) Your career. b) How many children you propose to have, and at what intervals. c) If you keep your career, how is the

rearing of children to be carried out? d) If you choose to make full-time motherhood your career, what shall be your compensation? e) What are the specific responsibilities and roles to be performed by each associate? f) What shall be the remedies and penalties, if any, in the event of a breach of the agreements? g) What shall be the conditions of termination, should either or both parties desire a termination of the contract?

* Plan the restoration of both partner's lives to a state as close as possible to what it would have been if either party continued their activities in the social strata had the marriage not taken place. For example, if the woman was pursuing a law career when she entered a marriage agreement, and gave it up for the benefit of the association, the association now has the responsibility of making it possible for her to resume on that path and, if possible, be compensated to the level she would have attained had she done so. Minimally, she should be given enough resources to bring her life to the degree of independence she would have enjoyed had she not entered the contract.

* Ensure that if you choose to abandon any of your personal security in favor of the association, such as your profession, there must be an agreement to not only compensate you for any new roles you will take in the association, such as the rearing of children, but also to permit the resumption of your financial freedom in the event of termination.

This subject calls for a workbook those contemplating such an association could consult as a guide, one which contains sufficient information to allow individuals to make informed decisions on the matter. Information exists on prenuptial agreements.

Many marital and post marital problems dealing with exchanges and fair mutual treatment exist because all these considerations and preparations have been viewed as rather silly and inconsequential. All these processes may seem to be a strenuous exercise. However, laws exist which are very unfavorable to one or another party in the marriage contract. In the face of the very visible social problems arising from unresolved disputes between partners, you will not think this precaution superfluous.

If you feel that negotiating such details before a marriage takes place is superfluous and unnecessary, as many do, a minimal rational precaution is at least to compare notes on principles that should apply in the event of dissolution.

Philosophical Digressions-Licenses, and Rights

A marriage license is curious thing when viewed in the same light of what might be called natural rights, vs. socially or legally granted rights.

I define natural rights as rights inherent to creatures by the very nature of their existence upon the face of the planet, such as the right to food, shelter, and other natural functions of living and procreating.

Licenses are rights granted by governments. We assume that governments are created, among other reasons, to protect our natural rights. As a general application, a license might be required on the premise that a) no natural right exists to engage in a given activity, and therefore a right to perform such activity must be granted by license; b) a natural right may demand licensing to protect the group or society from indiscriminate or harmful use of the natural right; c) licensing for the purpose of either granting special privileges or penalties, depending on what is socially desirable.

Here is an interesting distinction that acknowledges the difference: Under certain circumstances, hunting may be done without a license, and in such cases, it is permissible on the basis that the hunting is performed as a natural right to acquire food. When it is done for sport, however, it falls outside the concept of natural right and therefore becomes a right only by grant.

That line of thought implies that since a license is required for marriage, the law or the society does not see marriage as a natural right, or it sees it as an abused natural right, therefore requiring a license. Since it is obviously a natural right, we'd have to assume that licensing has been required to curb abuse, and privileges or penalties are required to be applied to the exercise of that natural right.

Abuse takes place as much under license than outside the scrutiny of licensing. That makes licensing for social protection spurious. Any benefits associated with the team effort of marriage and family, are nullified and set off to the negative by losses of social advantages through taxes, and other inequitable laws, which clearly penalize the association. What then is the benefit of acquiescing to obtain a license?

Marriages That Work

It would be unfair to suggest that a relationship that looks like marriage or is a marriage in either a romantic or a social sense, will never work. While researching and reviewing marriages that work, I found what I loosely classify into two general areas: The religious philosophy marriages and the social philosophy marriages.

I define work as passing the accomplishing set objectives test: Lifetime connection, nurturing and reasonably stable survival of the family.

In the first category, an outstanding example comes to mind of a rabbi, his wife, and children who I was privileged to visit many times. There, I observed the members in a close, loving, connection, and in their presence I felt an aura that emanated warmth and good feelings. In that particular family there is so much love and harmony that one can't help being deeply moved.

In the second category, arranged marriages, I found that while they did not contain the high level of warmth one might expect, the solidarity was clear, and the mutual support and cooperation was visible. There was a very significant rate of success in prearranged marriages, regardless of social settings or other ethnic aspects.

Upon observing these workable marriages, I saw a prenuptial and continued understanding of

* Purposes and objectives of the union
* Common realities and agreement on key matters
* Clearly understood roles
* An unshakable commitment to fulfill agreements to that creation

These were not conditions placed upon the connection at the time of the declaration of commitment, but were strongly held realities, whether religious, social or otherwise. In other words, they knew what they were getting into, and were in agreement with those ideals before the public declaration of their vows. Whether the tenacity honoring the commitment was born out of duty or personal conviction, it was sufficiently powerful to hold the connection in place and thriving within their own purposes and objectives.

The brevity of this section should not be interpreted as dismissive. On the contrary, the purpose of this section is to emphasize that currently existing workable relationships have many of the ingredients I am attempting to help you create with the concepts presented in this book.

The point in these observations of marriages that work is to illustrate that their workability contains some of the same major ingredients discussed in this book.

It is often said that wisdom is only attainable in the face of adversity. This has proven to be true many times. I have acquired the most enduring and profitable lessons during periods of severe challenge, failure and struggle, and invariably have come out the other end shattered and exhausted, but after a few days' rest and recuperation I was restored and revitalized, ready to take on newer and bigger challenges than before, and with new certainty and self assuredness. Those of us who have gone through this crucible, and know the visitation of the hell as a result of break ups, understand why this is the Wisdom phase. So, before you have a chance to indulge in sorrows of desperation until you lose yourself, hold on to the awareness that when it's all over, you can still have won!

Part VI
Wisdom

Love is the emblem of eternity: it confounds all notion of time: effaces all memory of a beginning, all fear of an end.
~ Germaine De Stael ~

Chapter Nineteen
The Breakdown of Marriage

As you follow the progress of this book you will have come to see the cycle of a connection from the instant of meeting, through all the intervening steps, to the shoals and narrows. Having survived that, it progresses to a successful nurturing phase, and continues its growth toward greater sharing, intimacy, trust, and all the desirable aspects of the connection.

Here is the anatomy of the process of relationships. Well managed, it takes this path:

Coming together   agreement   sharing   joint action   greater agreement   commitment   nurturing   success   success. At any given time in this cycle a disagreement can take place, and if unresolved it marks the beginning of a breakdown of the connection that ends, sometimes years later, in irreconcilable issues.

As a result the process will travel this path:

Disagreement   distancing   independent action /violation of agreement   secrecy   apprehension   mistrust   rationalizations and justifications, fault finding

This diagram is a very clear schematic of the basic progression sequence in a breakdown of a connection. The cycle may start, but it will not necessarily end in a breakdown if corrective action is taken at any point in its progression. This involves the interaction between two or more individuals. Each individual will move through the cycle in one of two general directions: one, passive; the other, active. When passive, the individual has a disposition toward the cessation of motion, inactivity, and withdrawal. When active, the individual has a disposition toward extroversion and action, that is, actual deeds or decisions resulting in actions.

When people agree or realize they have a common reality, a certain affinity, liking, or closeness takes place. When there is a disagreement which does not resolve through conflict resolution or any other method, the reverse takes place; there is an immediate distancing between the persons involved, the affinity is broken. This is loosely followed by an almost automatic attitude that one must remain independent, and act alone on at least that particular issue. The impasse may cause inactivity (passive) or independent action (active) on an issue where there had been a previous agreement to act in consultation. The action is a violation of agreement against the association. If the action is not kept a secret, there still exists a possibility of resolution. However, there is a high propensity for secrecy in most cultures, so such actions are generally kept a secret.

On the passive side, the person transgressed against very frequently will sense the shift in the connection and will feel apprehension and some measure of mistrust, which prompts one to start looking for signs of transgressions.

If the secret is not discovered or communicated, the transgressor instantly feels the need to separate further. That is the direct result of the secrecy. To explain the separation, transgression, and treason, the person will assert as a valid rationale for the action one or more deficiencies on the other person's part.

Petty matters, not a prior issue, now become major ones that justify the secret and treasonous act. More frequently, things which took place after the transgression and the secrecy are cited as reasons for the treachery. It's the he-hit-me-first syndrome so frequently used by children, wherein the reason for the transgression actually took place after the

Chapter Nineteen — The Breakdown of Marriage

transgression. In cases where the reason for the transgression took place before it, it is invariably something that was originally not an issue. Now, the transgressor declares it an issue in retrospect to use as a justification. It is turned into an issue after the fact.

Treason and treachery might be seen as harsh words, even in these circumstances. They are not harsh, they are amply appropriate, as they describe what took place: Treason or treachery violates a trust. The trust is either an implicit or explicit agreement of behavior that was in place prior to the act. It is not whether the action was a good or bad action; it's that it was a violation of a real or assumed trust, and real or assumed agreement.

This progresses through more independent action further violation of agreements more mistrust more distancing more severe accusations of wrong-doing, to the point of fabrication of reasons further distancing closing down of all communication termination of the connection obsession, guilt, blame, shame, regret, oblivion proportionate to the degree of refusal to own up to one's own responsibility and actions.

Obsession may assail both parties to one degree or another during this tug-o-war. Oblivion is the state of total loss of memory of any connection having existed at all. Any memory of it has vague unreality, and they are often false memories.

This entire cycle can become so confusing for the untrained observer that it may even look utterly implausible.
Why and how does the first disagreement that sets off the cycle take place? Everyone enters a life activity with a fairly complete set of realities and notions considered irrevocable truths. When one of these realities clashes with another, both individuals tend to become rigid about what they know is true, and right there they create an impassable barrier, which is the separation that sets the cycle in motion.

An irreconcilable impasse invariably blocks any real future progress, and is eventually the seed of a breakup.
Who's Fault is it?

We know breakups happen; we know we are usually devastated when they break up with us. We know we can devastate another when we break up with them. Finally, we don't know whether we will recover.

Sometimes the breakup was undertaken for the survival of the person breaking away, either from abuse or other severely intolerable conditions. Even under these circumstances it often recoils on the person who decides to depart. Much of the anguish and pain is not so much from the actual separation from the person who victimized one, but from the separation from the expectations and dreams one had counted on, oh, so strongly for so long a time, and from the conflicts between what one believed and the reality one is now experiencing. Memories of promises of bliss and happiness come crashing onto one's head with a tremendous weight. The memories seem to belie the experience of love in the connection.

What is even more incomprehensible is the fact that the severance of all communication, and the total disconnection with another with whom you had been deeply bonded, is such an unnatural event that it recoils on both parties.

Let's say you are the person who has been left. How does it recoil on the other side? They experience similar pain and anguish. But since they have what they see as a plausible reason for the breakup, the pain and anguish is not caused by the incomprehensibility of the breakup.

The departing party tends to appear slightly more emotionally stable than the abandoned one. They know the reasons, and they have had plenty of opportunity to create them to ensure they are doing something that they feel perfectly justified in doing. The departing party feels pain and anguish due to the mechanical effects of the shifts in the energies in the relationship. The reason is rarely the true underlying cause of their departure. It may be an actual event in real life, but not a true cause. The pain and anguish therefore will be necessarily repressed, as an automatic assertion of rightness: "See, the reasons I left were valid. I am happier and feel better now." This is subjective, and an observer can only ascertain its veracity upon an evaluation of the broader area of the person's life; if there is a clear degradation of the person's life, it is a fair assumption that repressed pain and anguish is underneath.

Nothing in the aforesaid is intended to attribute an intrinsic rightness or wrongness in the actions themselves. Moreover, such attribution can only be evaluated against the underlying objectives to which the actions are taken. The person, who has been left, tends to blame self, and analyze forever as to what might have been done wrong and how some other action might have been better. Those errors are not the cause of the break up, whether they existed or not. The cause is always the actions of the departing party, who invariably uses the other party's actions as a justification. Fleeing from severe abuse is possibly the only exception to this assertion.

Finally, there is a rather common truth that is often overlooked: With the possible exception of break ups from abuse or other severely intolerable conditions, a rather common truth is the secret or un-communicated reasons why the person entered into the connection in the first place. This has been referred to as the wrong reason for getting together in the first place. This wrong reason, usually a purely selfish one, has been kept secret, and is often the root truth as to why the person ends up leaving.

Here is an example I recently came across:

Alice was having problems in her job, and was about to get fired because of poor performance. She was looking for a way out, and had a couple of lovers that might just give her the ticket to free herself from the job before she got fired. Lover number one consented to take Alice into his home and make a life and a future with her. Unbeknownst to lover number one, Alice was in intimate communication with lover number two, whom she had told was the love of her life. When lover number one opened his doors to her, she dropped the job as fast as she could, disappeared from lover number two's life, and moved in with lover number one.

The beginning was fine, as it usually tends to be. But within a few months, she had a package of completely new, yet repetitive problems of the type she was attempting to run from upon leaving her job: anguish, confusions, inner conflicts, and all the sensations in the body that accompany the uncertainties that she carried.

She resolved these problems by continuing to look for yet another way out, and carried on several secret communications with others, while living with lover number one. Finally, she had an opportunity to leave, and did so, leaving lover number one, cutting all communication with him, and going to live with one of the two new lovers she had been nurturing.

The original wrong reason for joining lover number one set the stage for the secret behavior that followed. Once lover number one discovered and understood the truth, hard as it may have been to accept, the anguish left him, and he was able to move on.

Regardless of the reason for the breakup, the focus must now be placed on healing. One has suffered such a deep loss that the pain has to end. It's time for the healing process to begin.

Basis for Repair

The reasons the contract came into existence were clearly established earlier in the book. It ensures a level of enforcement and continued clarity of agreements. It also ensures that if there is a breach, the parties can call each other on the matter, and achieve the necessary negotiations to cure any discrepancies, often describing by what means conflicts are to be resolved. Sometimes it contains penalties for breaches and methods of termination where a cure cannot be attained. If the contract doesn't resolve the dispute, then appeals can be made to third parties and the courts. Many elements of a

Chapter Nineteen — The Breakdown of Marriage

marriage contract that will be enforced by courts of law are written in law books. These laws differ from place to place. I do not know of an instance where those about to marry ever receive or see these laws, and the penalties connected with their violation. So by the time it has come to the courts or an arbiter, the marriage is rarely salvageable, and the absence of a prior understanding of said laws is a major contributor to the dispute.

Let me present you with a couple of scenarios:

Business Conflict Resolution Session:

    Arbitrator: Can I see a copy of your contract? (He is handed a copy of the contract, and reads it.) Very well! Explain your positions. (Each side presents the issues)
Now, based on the recorded agreements, the arbitrator can be clearly aware of the breaches by either or both parties. The job is simple. He tells side A his perception of the breach, and asks: "If you don't agree, can you pose your concept of the breach?" Getting both parties to recognize or rephrase their extent of the breach is not difficult at all. From that recognition, the arbitrator can easily construct a compromise remedy for both sides, and the whole process takes just a few hours. If the arbiter applies the law, then it's a simple matter of his interpretation and educated judgment. No other considerations need to be taken into account, but often are for the benefit of the parties.

Now, here is another scenario:

    The counselor asks each of the parties what are their concepts of the agreements on which the marriage is based. This process alone has taken weeks just to get some fairly consistent common idea of the existing or original agreement. Rarely are they on the same basis. And even more rare is their ability to come to terms about the differences. Each believed, and continues to believe, that what they related was actually the contract under which they were supposed to live.

Needless to say, that without these underpinnings, there is nothing to resolve. There is no contract. I've succeeded in repairing, temporarily, such vague sets of conflicting agreements. However, the parties, always go back to the extreme positions they held at the beginning of the consultation. That is reason enough to make it nearly impossible to fix a marriage, since the underlying agreements are not clearly known and agreed upon by the involved parties.
There are two obvious paths: One toward restoration of the connection, and one toward oblivion.

Restoring a Foundation

If the reason for the marriage was the result of unconditional love that bloomed at the beginning of the connection, based on a long-term, strong foundation of common realities and agreements and a great deal of love, there is a remote possibility that this can be restored. I say remote because the conflicts that have come to create the breach in the first place may have created a chasm too difficult to bridge.

Yet, he keeps calling, and she keeps yearning for him. In their conversations they continue to swear undying love for each other. He says he wants back in, she says she does too, but cannot live the kind of life they lived together. She's already given it several tries. They lived together several times and broke up again.

First, a clear choice to salvage or rebuild has to exist. If there is no true intent to repair and rebuild the connection, no attempt will work. Second, the criteria for resolution should be restoration of the connection to the optimum state it had once been. Third, the notion that once in that state, the individuals can reevaluate the connection and reestablish a direction, whether it be a continuation or a transition into a different state or different set of agreements, changing the nature of the connection to a different form. Whatever the outcome, the parties to the connection must be in enthusiastic agreement with it.

Chapter Nineteen

The Breakdonw of Marriage

When love is not madness, it is not love.
~Pedro Calderon de la Barca~

Chapter Twenty
The Road Back

Will anyone whose marriage has been saved through counseling and arbitration please stand up! I have considered the enforcement of a marriage contract disqualified as viable method of salvage. It can only serve an arbiter to make equitable disposition of the wreckage.

A few thousand words and more could be written on the road back to the high point of a connection, which would cover the complexities, subtleties, and nuances into which people can take this simple concept:

A total, uncensored revelation of all actions must be opened to the other party in the connection; a complete owning up of one's actions must take place, and it must be with a cold blooded sense of one's own inner motivations, without an attempt at softening or reducing responsibility by believing, pretending, or declaring one's actions to be motivated by the actions of another. Actions are the direct result of intentions.

This idea is highly unpopular, and the first reaction I get when I mention it is, "What about accidents?" Not before people have been in enough accidents and recognize their own point of intention, decision, and action that contributed as cause to the accident, will the idea begin to gain some acceptability.

Even in abusive situations we are confronted with the concept that the abused person is a complete victim. Relief from having been a victim of abuse can only finally be attained when the victim finds and can own up to some level of causative contribution to the abuse. The moment one's own point of cause is discovered, the abuse often stops because the discovered volitional or causative action of the abused can now cease.

Obviously an infant is unable to physically defend itself against physical abuse, but the recovery in therapy can only happen when, in retrospect, the now adult victim discovers some element of causation on his part. This sounds a bit far fetched. Nevertheless, I would like to present two points which support its validity. One is that the healing has actually taken place by the adult's discovery of his participatory cause to the action, whether real or imagined. It may be purely subjective creation by the adult, but its therapeutic value cannot be denied. The second is a recollection many individuals undergoing therapy have noticed. In recalling childhood events, many have related to an experience of a dual memory; one as a helpless child undergoing a trauma, the other, as a hovering entity, with an all knowing sense of being in full control, and knowledge of the events taking place.

Thus, ability to recognize and admit cause is the key to the recovery process in removing the distance that was created with the first unresolved disagreement, which then prompted independent action, keeping secret those actions, and intentions. The most important action is to remove those barriers; by revealing the actions and then clearing up the disagreement.

Mark and Donna met and were swept by a whirlwind of excitement, passion. The connection evolved through understandings and common realities, high sense of common purpose and agreement, and eventually to a lifetime commitment. A few months down the line, things were not as high as they were the first two weeks after they'd made their commitment. They began by attempting to address issues. Primarily, Donna had a series of issues and points about Mark that she was having second thoughts about.

The confrontation of issues did not bring them any closer. In fact, the more issues they handled, the more Donna came up

Chapter Twenty — The Road Back

with yet to be handled. Donna began to act as though she was independently taking unilateral action on matters that affected the connection. Finally, Donna announced that she had decided she wanted to be alone, as she had been for such a long time. She had Mark move out, and for the subsequent months the conversations got more and more strained, with a great deal of blame, and shame. Eventually, they stopped talking, and didn't see each other again. That is one possible ending.

In another scenario, let's say Mark was given the miraculous opportunity to go back to a point where there was still some semblance of communication. He said to Donna that before any further discussion on issues were to take place, she had to tell all that she had been hiding or keeping secret, and anything she felt he would not approve.

With much patience, even to the point of badgering, Mark practically cornered Donna into admitting she had been talking to a former lover, and was very much in love with him. This is a good step. However, she was sure she was doing the right thing because of the love she had for this other man. She couldn't help herself for loving him so. Mark allowed her to say all she felt, and she revealed the private plans she had been making to meet and recreate with her former lover. Nevertheless, being helplessly in love was the key justification and rationalization; therefore, Donna was acting out an addiction. An addition can be generally defined as an action one takes which is purportedly completely outside our control. For our intents and purposes this is obsession.

Mark asked Donna to write down everything that she would say her lover, and everything she had said to him; specifically things Donna was unwilling to have Mark hear, no matter how innocent. After that was complete, Mark read it and coached Donna into looking for points where she intended and put into action those intentions, including the intention to love. After Donna discovered her own intentions and the way she went about implementing them, she was able to own up to all her actions. The affinity was restored and the issues vanished. The connection returned to its former highest point. They addressed the disagreement that had set off the breakdown cycle without any difficulty.

The recovery process took several months, but when it was completed, both knew that it was completed and handled totally, and would not repeat. The former lover vanished and made no further attempts to contact Donna.

This is a highly accelerated and simplified process. In reality, the handling can be arduous and at times impenetrable. The real secrecy crucible is hard to discover because love is such a highly socially acceptable reason to betray that we generally stop at that point, thinking it's terribly reasonable. There are many other socially acceptable excuses which close the door on ever discovering the underlying truths, that it is no wonder there are rarely true recoveries after a break up. While not completely acceptable socially, lies, deception and secrecy are strongly condoned, and often protected as a personal right.

In order for this to process succeed, a great deal of preparation is necessary, as covered in earlier chapters, including, and with greater emphasis to "The Hidden, Dark Self."

I endured and survived my share of personal breakups by the time I began this book, and have successfully applied these concepts. The resolution of the pain and anguish connected with a breakup is a complete understanding of all of the hidden aspects of the situation. The truth is usually very simple, usually down to a very early hidden motive. Knowing what falsehood had been injected into the situation became unimportant. Often the truth can be discovered in the falsehoods that are presented. That is, when you are told a lie, the content of the lie itself will point to a truth, which is intended to remain hidden. They are easy to recognize, and usually the clearest signs are one's own emotional responses. The level of anguish and apprehension tends to rise instantaneously when one is presented with a falsehood. There could be many falsehoods, all neatly and intelligently supported with the correct rationalizations; there is only one truth. When you hit upon the truth, some or all the anguish vanishes.

How can one discover the truth? Let me stress that actions are the result of intentions entertained in the mind. This is the most important signal. I think there also is a natural sense for truth. It requires that one be willing to be hit with whatever the truth is. Truth in these matters becomes a rather personal thing, and experience can help toward understanding and sifting between truths and lies. You can ask and listen to the ideas of someone who may be in a better position to observe the situation from outside. However, you cannot solely rely on outside counsel. Beyond getting some guidance in where to look and how to handle some of your feelings, you have to use your faculties with determination. The personal truths that can bring you healing may appear quite strange to others, but they can be your salvation.

Agreements, Transgressions, Secrets, and Rationalizations

Agreements, transgressions, secrecy, and rationalizations have subtleties which, if not understood, will not be visible. That makes restoration impossible.
In addition to what is already normally understood in the meaning of these words, the nuances I discuss here are critical to the restoration process, since they are the ones that triggered or perpetuated the breakdown.

Tacit and everybody-knows agreements or transgressions:

An action a person knows the other will not approve of acts as a breach of agreement, a transgression. Feeling the need to think of a reason why an action one is about to take is not a violation of agreements is an indication that one believes it's a transgression of an existing agreement, whether expressed or unspoken. And the reason becomes the rationalization and justification.

Donna didn't expect a call from the former lover. However, when she talked to him, her desire to have had that former relationship work become stimulated, and instantly she rekindled that desire in her heart. So instantaneous is the reaction that she may not even be aware of having done so. Desire is the first act in the process of creating actualities in the physical realm.

Donna will not admit she recreated the desire at that moment. Yet, she then felt distanced from Mark. Mark felt the distance as well. Donna expressed to the former lover something quite innocent, "I wish things hadn't ended as they did between us. I was very much in love with you." This innocent statement slipped Donna's mind, and she made no mention of it to Mark. This was the beginning of innocent secrecy.

Donna's communication encouraged the former lover, and a few calls later Donna felt caught in a new web. She felt helpless, because she then believed she is still in love with him. Love then became the rationalization and justification for her transgression and secrecy. Failing to own her actions, she behaved as someone who was suffering from an addiction. She no longer saw herself in control of her actions because that would have been tantamount to an admission of guilt and wrongdoing. She also began to find fault in Mark's behavior in order to explain her distancing. His faults were the reason she fell in love with someone else. There are many socially acceptable reasons that can be used to relieve oneself of the responsibility of a transgression. This is one of the most important reasons why many connections cannot be fixed.

There are about as many subtleties as there are circumstances of agreements, transgressions, secrets, and justifications/rationalizations. If these are missed, the attempt at recovery will fail.

Underneath this whole puzzle, fear is the basic reason a person feels the need or compulsion to commit a transgression. Real or imagined, fear for one's survival and security demands an act of self-defense. This element of fear is likely something that has been with the person since an early age,

Chapter Twenty *The Road Back*

and has little or nothing to do with the current relationship, aside from the fact that something in it will have triggered the insecurity.

If a recovery fails, the only thing left is salvage!

For every beauty there is an eye somewhere to see it.
For every truth there is an ear somewhere to hear it.
For every love there is a heart
somewhere to receive it.
~ Ivan Panin ~

Chapter Twenty One
Salvage Operation

    We have no choice but to ignore the departed lover, who has become unreachable, and possibly quite impenetrable to any communication. We must focus on keeping ourselves healthy and on opening new roads. There are several options:
    If there is still communication and the path to restoration of the committed state is not an option, and a private negotiated solution is not achievable, an arbitrated negotiation can still be a viable and graceful evolution.
If there is no easy way of agreement, an arbitrated solution will most likely take care of any logistic arrangements and division of property. This is unavoidable fallout from the dissolution of a connection, marriage, or other forms of commitment.
    Often at this point one realizes it would have been a simple task to have a written contract at the beginning, and it would diminish the anguish connected to the process. A review of a simple contract of commitment at this point has on a number of occasions provided enough resolve to make it possible to achieve a restoration of that commitment.
    In the absence of such a contract, the general advice with regard to material things is to be as generous as you can. Make it possible for new beginnings to be as easy as possible. If the connection was not established in a well planned manner, as suggested earlier, it is advisable to be respectful, kind and generous to each other.

Our main concern, however, in this book is the emotional, mental, and spiritual state after the break up. The end of a relationship rarely takes place gracefully. Yet, if viewed as an evolving, necessary change in the course of life, it can be approached with more sanity than we've been accustomed to.

Emotional Turbulence

Rebuilding a life after a break up can be a significantly difficult task, taking, in many cases, many years. And sometimes there is no rebuilding. The wounds are so deep and severe that the individuals see no healing in sight. The clock has been stopped at the precise moment the person began to regret the events of the break up, and is now attempting with a mental effort to keep them from coming to pass. Yet, there is life at the other end of a break up. There is healing.

During the management of the logistics of life rearrangements, and long after, there is an underlying low intensity background of mental and emotional loss which can plague one for a long time.

Loss of the connection to loved ones seems almost unavoidable, especially in our social settings, which seem to grant many acceptable reasons for break ups and departures, not to mention the economic pressures that force them. The anguish connected to such losses can be quite devastating. It has frequently led to suicide. The anguish is accompanied by some excruciating sensations in the body, the feeling of emptiness, the incomprehensibility of it all, the feelings of inadequacy, of self-blame. All of this is quite confusing. You are immobilized, hearing in your mind the words told you. "I've decided to spend the rest of my life with another person I have found."

Regret evokes the continuous hope and desire that something will happen that will change everything back to the way things were. One is assaulted by ideas that create the impulse to take action because one continuously discovers new reasons for the break up, which one can now repair. Then the desperation returns, and one begins to pine away and die a bit more each day; only days ago you were told never had they been so close to anyone in their entire life than with you. Now they've found someone to be closer to. All this simply doesn't make sense.

We compare what we have to what we had envisioned our connection was to become. It never did, but we continued to believe that it could and it eventually would. Our hopes had been so high, and we'd so vividly envisioned it, that the breakup is utterly incomprehensible, and cruel; it escapes our understanding, and leaves a large hollow space inside which brings a great deal of sorrow. We are continuously triggered into remembering random events of the connection—reading a letter, hearing a voice, seeing the person at a distance—all these things will bring the attention to the loss and to the pain.

We keep looking back to what we might have done to avert the painful outcome, and we look back to try to discover what we might have done to bring it on. This goes on and on, endlessly. This is a time when no amount of advice, soothing words, commiseration, or compassion will heal you, much less take your attention from your sorrow.

I recommend you do the healing exercises and meditations suggested in order to achieve some level of comfort and clarity. It may yet happen that the connection evolves into a warm friendship, and memories of pleasant times, and wonderful learning.

Recovery & Healing Exercises

It is difficult to focus on recovery amidst the pain and sorrow one might be undergoing. Reading this section will bring about some distraction and some comfort. When you are a bit more relaxed, and have achieved a bit of calm, review these concepts and try some of the exercises. They will help you out of the turbulence, and eventually heal you.

You need not have an objective for the meditations and drills beyond the desire to unburden yourself from the unpleasantness of the aftermath. Each of the meditations focuses on a specific emotional aspect of what is experienced in a breakdown of a relationship. You can determine in the healing process which emotional aspect is more important to resolve.

You will find your way around as you do the drills. I cannot hand you the answers. When I was a young man, my objective was never to feel these terrible feelings again. With time I've come to understand that they are part of the interchange of energies of life, and as important to life as good feelings. The objective became not to do away with the unpleasant feelings, but to understand them, and use them in moving toward growth, understanding, and creating a better next time. To this day I know I will anguish from a loss as I did as a young man. The anguish of the loss will burn the flesh today as it had in my youth. But today I fair it far better and resolve it much quicker using the tools in this book.

Comforting Connections

* Surround yourself with loved ones, family, and friends, and allow them to shower their affection upon you, and provide you with distraction, and comfort.
Time
* Allow time to pass before attempting any further communication with your former lover. Often the rancor and anger tend to return with some frequency during the healing period. There will be a proper time to re-establish communication, if it is necessary at all or even desirable.
Eradicating Regret and Focus on Events
* Try to let go of any mental effort to stop the breakup from happening. Often anguish becomes stronger from the mere effort to stop the break up. In order to let go, you allow yourself to experience the break, and let it flow. That is, let it have happened. You actually move the events mentally along the time stream, acknowledging that they have indeed taken place. Do this until you can embrace it all as an acceptable

experience from which you will draw knowledge and even pleasure. If you feel an overwhelming loss and sinking feeling, simply explore it and experience it. Gently focus on the events, and have them be okay.

Distractions

* Distractions. It is important to do things that demand attention to such a degree that they will make the loss take a place in the background. Going out with friends, working, or dating others are good distractions.

Focusing on the Feeling

* An inevitable alternative is to focus on the loss. This would seem inappropriate, since you're trying to forget. Yet, there is a special way of focusing wherein you simply allow your attention to settle and feel those aspects of the loss which appear intolerable. You might try this when the pressure from the loss is such that even distraction doesn't work; you find that the pain from the loss steals productive time; you cannot do your work, nor concentrate on other responsibilities. The loss lingers in the background and in the foreground of your mental processes. This is when you go for a walk, and simply feel what is going on.

Because the connection to the pain via the process of feeling is very powerful in lifting the pain, within moments your attention will be diverted to other thoughts. It may also be that the pain is so intense, that your attention is almost forced away from the pain. In both circumstances, try to refocus on the pain or uncomfortable feeling. In either case you will notice that something will change with a brief look and feel at the pain. Do this focusing for 15 to 20 minutes each day. This type of focusing is directed on the feeling, not on the event. When doing this exercise, you may perceive the feeling as a general area of discomfort which seems to have an actual physical shape, mass, color, and other attributes of a physical object. Observe these attributes, and reexamine the size frequently, since observation will cause it to change, and seeing it as it is at any given moment will cause it to change, and eventually disappear.

Relieving Obsession

> * Relieve any emotional obsession that might be present with the exercise given in the "Easing and Relieving Obsession," section
> * The section "The Road Back" prescribed various actions to bring the truth of the situations into the open. It is obviously difficult to try to obtain the truth from someone who has disappeared. However, those actions can still be done solo, and they will provide enough truth to free one from the unknowns, and the incomprehensibility of the events. Since the other party is not there to respond, you can fill in the answers from educated guesses, suppositions, and extrapolations drawn from the experiences which took place during the time spanning the relationship, from the beginning to the end.

Truth

> "Know the truth, and the truth shall set you free." We have often come to understand this concept in an entirely different manner. Let's apply the meaning not just to concepts of imponderable deep truths about existence and the creation of the universe, but also to the truth of the every day life, the small, subtle truths that drive the minds and actions of men.
> The exercise or meditation on the discovery of truth restores the self confidence that may have been stolen from a belief that it was your wrong actions which caused the break up, when in fact, the person who left did so as a result of their own thinking and considerations based on their evaluations of the circumstances, despite the fact they have continued to accuse you and your actions to be the reasons for their de-

parture. But you are already well aware of what your actions were. What you are interested in achieving in this process is the knowledge of the actions and intentions of the other person that were kept secret, and were never revealed to you.

People generally believe that it is impossible to know what's in the heart and mind of the person that has left, and the private or secret reasons they hold in their heart about their departure. I've chosen not to accept that as a fact. So I have pursued understanding with tenacity. The pursuit of the truth has always provided me with answers.

I make an unqualified generalization, and I'm asserting proof that sounds very much like a self-fulfilling prophecy. Discovering the truth does indeed set one free. If one has not achieved freedom, one has not discovered the truth. This may appear incredibly subjective. It can be that a subjective truth is sufficiently acceptable as to allow one to let go. The incomprehensible confusions tied to the breakup, which continue to invade, and anguish your mind, are immersed in falsehoods. Once the truth is discovered and understood, the anguish comes to an end. This discovery is an internal one, but it can also involve the discovery of the true thoughts and feelings in the hearts and minds of others involved in the breakup. All of the drills and meditations given in this section allow the truth to dawn upon one's consciousness. They have thoroughly hidden the truth and are proceeding to prove the uprightness of their falsehood. Often they are not aware of their own feelings with the degree of clarity to be able to provide you such truth.

What you are told by them isn't always verifiable. There is no way to prove or disprove that what you have been told about the breakup, is either true or false; therefore, sometimes it appears impossible to understand why people break up with us. If you ever left someone you well may remember or realize now that you could not provide the other person with a truly understandable and completely truthful explanation. As a result you often have to stand on your own senses. The anguish and confusion does, however, resolve when you discover the truth, either internally or through real information. Conversely, it could be said that if the anguish persists, then not all the truth is yet known. The personal truth that can bring you healing could appear quite strange to others, but it can be your salvation.

Proactive Moves

* Until now, all events have been happening to you; you have been reacting. You are the receiving point of the action, and in a way you are the victim. A proactive step can be where you sever the connection. You can dissolve your side of the connection. Again, until now, you may have found yourself actively fighting and defending your position, reacting in anger, hatred, all in an effort to overcome not only the anguish and pain, but to turn back the loss, to stop it from happening. You may even have to take an action despite the understanding that initially it will not diminish the pain one bit.

Try writing a letter. Imagine and reconstruct the state of mind of how things were at the height of the relationship, when all looked so wonderful and endlessly blissful. From this state of mind, you can write a farewell; thanking the other person for the wonderful things they gave you, withdrawing any anger or rancor, reiterating your love, and your open door to them always.

The effect of such a letter is often therapeutic for both of you, if it merits being sent. It allows you to remove any bitterness that may have built up during the process of communicating the break up. If it is worthy of sending, it also has the potential of repairing the connection and may at times, rarely on an immediate basis, restore it to its original luster. Don't count on this (all secrets need to be cleared before anything else would work to rebuild the relationship).

Here is an interesting example that came across my desk; it is a letter written by a woman to a lover who abandoned her. It is an example of how the person undergoing what appeared to be a loss asserts what she feels is the beginning of her own acceptable truth.

Chapter Twenty One — Salvage Operation

"I want to thank you for the needed lesson and the needed growth that this blow has already brought me. I imagine that you were sent to me, and once you had sensed the deep sadness inside me you would know how to heal it Unwittingly, you caused the process to begin, for only someone into whose heart I had become part of so deeply and so quickly could have taught me such a lesson in such a short period of time.

My test was doubly cold and cruel, for when your first farewell arrived the trust had been broken in a small way, so I could have walked away without injury. Yet, you withdrew your farewell, and I chose to think that our ensuing more intimate voice contact had erased all confusions, and your genuineness suggested that the broken trust had been repaired, and you now were finally ready to explore what our future held.

Yes, this is my lesson, for I have to know how to come alive from such deep wounds I didn't even think myself vulnerable to, for I had thought I had experienced worse.
Perhaps I can repay the lesson with one you might benefit from:

Yesterday I spent the day tearing out the hurt from inside. This hurt can only come from the absence of truth. I hope you don't further dishonor me by coming to me trying to console me, for I don't need to be broken up with twice a day, day after day, and three times in one week, compounded with the betrayals of trust of broken promises.

You can think you know and have told me the truth, but that's not what you gave me. Don't come to me pretending that it is. Your actions, your decisions, are merely a strategy of life which you take either casually or thoroughly considered, but pure human strategy for living.

Yet, real love transcends all that. Once upon a time, people came to me expecting real, stable truths, and as a mystic, I have fixed myself in one position from which I could spout it, because they counted on my help and advice; at that point I discovered that my own search became stale. Nothing, however, is more illusive than truth and love. Why would I assume that you bring either? Or would even be capable of it?" The therapeutic value is in writing the letter. Not necessarily in having sent it or in it having been read by the other person. The writer believes and hopes that by pointing out what she sees as truth might help repair the connection. That is unlikely, since it is necessary that the recipient agree with that perception of the truth, a difficult thing to achieve when communication has been cut off (which was the case in this instance). It served more as an exercise in self healing. The connection was not repaired, but the writer felt quite relieved to have written it, to the extent that she understood certain truths. But let me repeat, there is little chance that any rebuilding will take place if the actions and secrets that broke it down are not revealed.

Talk to the Body

* Talk to the Body. This particular exercise may appear silly upon first impression. Nevertheless, it is quite effective in many cases. I came across this method when trying to take away a hurt when my little one suffered a minor injury. I would motion with my hand as if to physically grab and remove the hurt from the injured part of the body. In one or two passes, the hurt was gone! What is this all about?
Unexplainable painful emotion, apprehension, fear, and other feelings, register in the body as a physical sensation. This exercise or meditation works well most of the time:

* Mentally locate the area where the sensation or feeling appears to be.

* As best as you can, try to determine what it is. Imagine, for example, what shape, color, and other physical attributes that sensation appears to have.

* Talk to it like you would talk to a person. You might say, "Hello, how are you? What can you tell me about yourself?" There is any number of things you might say. Be honest and imaginative with your questions. Don't be shy about ask-

ing anything of this feeling or sensation.

*Receive its answer. Simply pretend or imagine that it is answering your questions. That is all. Listen to whatever answers you get, and let it know you understand.

* Do it until the uncomfortable sensation is significantly reduced, or until it will not diminish any further.

This is affective because the act of mentally focusing on something, engages nerve and brain activity. When talking to some hurt in the body, nerve signals travel from the brain to the body part one is talking to, setting some type of feedback and flow, which allows the nerve cells to carry the excess, locked up energy to discharge through the system.

Graceful Passage–Joseph's Dilemma

Biblical Joseph's brothers sold him to Egyptian slavery at an early age. Many years later, due to famine, their father sent them to Egypt to get food and provisions. They didn't recognize Joseph in the Egyptian official to whom they'd been taken to give them aid.

Would Joseph, remembering their treason, berate and punish them, denying them relief from the famine? Or would he rise above himself as the betrayed child, and come to the aid of his people?

Joseph could not have made the decision as a child to become an important Egyptian official, and would not have on his own accord left his father's side to go there. Did divine intervention require the use of the corrupt and unscrupulous hearts of his brothers' to accomplish its intent to send Joseph there? Was it the same divine intervention that helped him set revenge aside?

Joseph understood the higher purpose that brought him to Egypt in the first place was the salvation of his brethren, and of the twelve tribes that each would source, and expand throughout the world. He rose to see his role from the eyes of divinity, thus he became able to rise above his human desire for revenge.

We exercise our capabilities to control our actions, and to do the things we consider appropriate and correct for ourselves, our lives, the lives of our loved ones, and the benefit of the circle of life that surrounds us. Beyond our control, be they divine events or fortuitous coincidences, we receive them as either opportunities or misfortunes. We control our perception and opinion of them.

We are ready to start again. I've heard it cleverly expressed: "Love anew, as if you've never been hurt before."

Approach your life and your love in a sporting way. Make them into a game, intense, as you want, but a game just the same. This game is never lost unless you decide it's lost. It is only lost if you end it before it's over. You have not failed until you have stopped trying and making efforts to shape it the way you wish it to be.

Whether you heal or not is your decision. Don't allow the losses of your past to cripple you into inaction, and reticence to create love again. You may have been a victim of deception and treachery, but from your perspective the only things you can truly change are your own actions and habits. Therefore, you can do no more than work on sharpening your perceptions so you can see deception and treachery before it wounds you.

You must shoot to win, but don't get so obsessed with winning or you'll end up losing! The frame of mind that says, "I cannot live without him," can be the mental perspective and emotional emanation that will cause this round to be lost! Losing a round or two now and then is part of life. Get used to the idea of what it is like to have lost, and what will then be the alternative paths to continue. Consider the worse possible outcome, and thoroughly examine it. Prepare a plan of recovery as if the worse outcome is at hand, and review it until you feel comfortable that you will survive and move on successfully, should you lose this round. This process will also help to remove the anxiety of having to win, and immediately increase your chances of winning. Also, if it does come to pass that you lose, it will never be the worse possible outcome.

Chapter Twenty One — Salvage Operation

You'll already have a positive plan in place that can take you into the next part of the game.

Develop this analysis of your actions into a habit, and you will be relatively comfortable with your actions and potential maneuvers. After a while, you will notice you're living the attitude that you are likely to win on most rounds, and you will lead a relatively happy life.

In the final analysis, whatever the outcome, you have won. Didn't you want to connect to someone whose loyalty and endurance was to take your commitment for the rest of your life?

Freedom From Losing Patterns

We are in the Wisdom Phase. It's that stage of life where one will have achieved not only a level of understanding of connections, but may have come through several dramas of breakups, and acquired the wisdom to have renewed zest to take on new challenges, and win. As a result, one may be settled in the knowledge that one has a good grasp on how to make a relationship work.

Maybe we discover we have been through identical dramas again and again, repeating the same mistakes in very similar circumstances. The settings are the same. Time and again we are baffled to hear someone we know loves us deeply tell us they've chosen to spend their lives elsewhere. It would be easier to be told that they don't want to be with you because they hate you and find you unappealing, or even distasteful. We continuously enter into relationships we sense are doomed from the start.

What is happening? The reasons are rooted in our beliefs, in our mindset, and in our subconscious patterns and habits. That is why when we find ourselves going through similar types of relationships that begin, grow and end in very similar ways, it is time we review the roots of our inner selves to discover and break the pattern, and move our lives closer to the direction we want it to go.

When our ideas and beliefs have proven deficient, as evidenced by our perplexing confusions, shattered dreams, failures, or lack of knowledge and understanding, we are humbled. Suddenly we become open to new ideas and realizations. Pain and anguish often become the incentive to reach for higher understanding and wisdom.

For those whose relationships have survived, and are assured of a continued bliss, there is the continued enhancement of that connection, which in itself is a never-ending process.

For those who find themselves in tenuous situations, many things can be done to bring hope into the future, to create the sense that all is not lost. In the preceding sections and essays I discussed a variety of methods of freeing oneself from anguish and other undesirable effects of the deep wounds of loss.

One remaining important aspect to healing that must not be neglected is healing and correcting the patterns and root beliefs that set us up for repeated failures in the first place. It can be done through the application of many of the self-discovery drills and meditations in the Part I, in the New Ways to Love section; in Part IV, in the Violence and Abuse section, and the various drills and meditations in this chapter. Apply the drills and meditations with a slant, and focus on the elements forming the repetitive patterns you are able to define.

This process involves soul-searching procedures that delve into the past, and into the sources of fixed ideas, unshakable false beliefs, training patterns, and other habits. Since the sources of these patterns are often out of reach of one's usual ability to remember, (that alone a principal reason for their persistent influence), professional help is often desirable.

During this process the professional helps reach memories and truths that may have been hidden for years. These events are important because their impact on a person's reality is very powerful, and tends to shape new realities. The person's decisions and conclusions at the time of these events are also important aspects of shaping his reality. The events we are usually looking for are incidents that have taken place during times of high vulnerability and uncertainty. The unknown elements in those events affect the individual in unpredictable ways. The professional will assist in recovering principles and realities formed during such moments of high vulnerability, thereby freeing one from the influence of the decisions and conclusions drawn during such moments.

I am intentionally avoiding the use of the term psychotherapy since I don't want to suggest that psychotherapy is neither the only way nor even a workable way of recovering self. There are professional psychotherapists who are able to help, but there are other professionals in other healing arts who are equally and sometimes more competent. In choosing professional help, you should talk to other people who have been helped by the person whose help you are considering engaging. Length of practice may be important, and if the professional has written about his area of expertise, his writings may clearly show you whether he is the person you can trust to help you.

Of particular value are the Reality Adjustment exercises in Part I, Chapter Three. These can be worked alone or with the help of a friend who clearly understands the purpose of the meditation. All the drills, exercises and meditations can be done alone, or with the coaching or assistance of friend. In very difficult situations they can be done with the help of a professional. Any review, even of what may appear superficial, will begin to crack the pattern enough to get one moving forward, and with hope.

Among the many other things with which we deal, the application of the theories and exercises in this little manual and the processes for healing and restructuring past destructive patterns, allowed us to:

1. Release fears from our consciousness which cause the urge to depart or otherwise sabotage relationships. In the instance of one example, this was traced to an incident of rape.

2. Retrieve the guilt in several other events of abuse,

as contained in important moments when the conviction of one's own badness is discovered.

3. Remove the shame and guilt over pleasure the person felt, even as a victim of abuse. It is very easy to dismiss the importance pleasure can play in the wounds of abuse. The idea of pleasure seems utterly unbelievable on the face of it, until you have actually discovered it. It may be difficult to reveal this aspect without assistance, but not impossible. At the same time, it must not be assumed that there will always be pleasure in events of abuse. But if it is an underlying presence, it must be discovered before shame can be removed.

4. Repair relationships when early signs of a breakup begin to arise.

After the healing, one woman wrote this to me:

"I never thought I could have loved again. As the healing process was progressing, my perceptions and attitudes changed. Then, it felt that the healing had opened new doors. I found a man who listened to me, who respected me, one whom I began to like, and enjoy.

Yet, it was I who had changed. I was finally able to find a man who would fill me with love. I came to understand that it was actually easy to love and be loved, as long as I let myself do so.

Having rid myself of the ghosts of the past that made love impossible, I was once again able to love deeply, openly and honestly, and, above all, without fear of loss.
Love was and is within me, and I felt the confidence that love depends on me and how I love, and only secondarily upon the other person being sufficiently aware to know the same.
This process not only brought out of me how to love, but this time, how to love openly, honestly, truthfully and to give all to the love that I felt."

If nothing else, this woman sees life in a brighter more hopeful light. At this time, can we ask for more?
First Love The Second Time Around

Chapter Twenty One — Salvage Operation

You have come this far, and have learned all the sorrows and ecstasies of connections. You have learned to rise above, and survived the wounds of the sorrows. From wisdom gained, you have a set of rules listing what to avoid, what to ask for, and what to ensure, before ever again stepping into an intimate connection.

You have reexamined losing repetitive patterns successfully; you will have thrown away many rules that you have come to know as unworkable. In that process of reexamination you will have resolved on some new rules. Armed with new wisdom and with the useful tools provided you in this manual, you can now truly handle the difficulties of past heartbreaks, and pains and sorrows, and "Love like you have never been hurt before."

The first love is never forgotten. With the memories of it, now refreshed with new energies and new life, free from anguish and fears, you can take the time to create a new first love far superior to the memory of your first love. The power and innocence of the first love contrasted to the second first love should create hope to move forward, despite all fears.

Songs and tales of first love abound. It's generally believed that nothing will ever be as good. I would like to assure you that nothing is further from the truth. I have achieved this for myself, and have helped many reach the ecstatic state of first love the second time around. Healing through these simple drills and common sense methods has produced pleasantly surprising results:

"I have been going through life from one adventure to the next hoping to find the relationship that would be like my first love that for some unhappy set of circumstances fell apart when I was twenty three. Finally, at the age of forty, I was sure that opportunity was gone forever. With the concept of unconditional love, as I read it in an unpublished manuscript of this book, unattainable as it may sound, it was practicable. It made a significant impact that brought a change into my life, and I know that I have reached my first love again. I dare say it's more than my first love could ever have been."

The first love should not be downgraded to puppy love (a love without any real meaning, the flavor of the word itself puppy lessens the value of that love), nor should one suggest that it was all a reaction to a biological need. In the presence and force of the biological urge, sexual activity rarely takes place without something more. Let me bring your attention once again to the magic key. The qualities of the magic key seem to be readily alive in the young. Children are more readily able to give, allow, and embrace completely.

Is the first love less vulnerable to the booby traps of any other relationship? It is vulnerable primarily because of the booby traps in the social environment and the abundance of deception that can be encountered therein. Lack of understanding can cloud one's perceptions of who others are.

I think you are now equipped to create your first love, a second time, and in ways you might have never imagined before.

Love is Where You Build It- New Frontiers

When you consider the high rate of dissolution of marriage contracts, the repeated traumas of failed connections, and the loneliness from the fear to try it again, it is obvious that there are many people stranded in some social limbo.

But there is healing; and after healing there is a lot more to explore. I could have included many stories of how broken lives and broken hearts have been rebuilt as if a phoenix from the ashes. I've refrained from including more personal stories because they are not mine to reveal. In those personal stories, and in stories that have yet to come, there are those who have thought themselves to be on the threshold of death, yet have come to discover new life with fresh ideas. They have dared explore new possibilities, new loves, and new life.

For many the healing takes place late in life. But it is never too late to reach new heights. Love the second time around takes on a new meaning as you approach to know and sense the unity of body, mind, and spirit, as different hues of the same spectrum. New levels of intimacy are reached through a clearer understanding of this life spectrum.

There is the exploration of a deeper power of sex, and its connection to the creative force. When the procreative activity begins to ebb, some aspects of sex come into view. These aspects are usually overlooked in earlier years, when sex is at some stage of social practice often seen as a sport. Sex is viewed by most predominantly as an important way of communicating love.

Sex has been held as a sacred activity in many religions and philosophies of the world. The mystical aspects of sex are beginning to be explored in some modern civilizations. Tantric and Sexual Magic are among such practices and studies. Many books exist on the subject. They central theme revolves around the use of the sexual and love energy to achieve enlightenment or for personal gratification or attainment of personal desires.

There are some important things which to me are not clearly detailed in any of the books I have read on the subject, although the basic premise merits consideration, I believe there are things which can easily be misleading. Most commonly misleading is the great importance given to sexual positions. Mystical and spiritual practices are often filled with rituals. The rituals have their usefulness. Rituals are repeated actions, motions, and rhythms which are intended to stimulate in the mind the concepts contained in the meaning ritual have come to acquire through practice and tradition.
For example: the spreading of opened arms toward the sky, as a gesture to funnel divine energy. The symbolic value of the gesture or ritual, when subscribed to, can stimulated the mind or the spirit to create a strong sense of reality that such divine energy is being evoked.

The focus on sexual positions can easily become an over concentration on a ritual.

The sexual act behaves like a trigger of a wide range of emotions and powers, which are not yet clearly understood. At an earlier age, sex triggers enough creative energy to produce children. This is rarely understood because pregnancy occurs at random. However, this energy can be monitored and converted into other than children. I don't believe this is understood well enough to be practical.

Later in life, when children are neither a possibility nor a desire, the creative energies that can be experienced are much stronger when there is active attention in such exploration. Manifestations of such exploration in a non-bearing portion of life are the increase of the creative energy, and the separation of the ritual from the energy. That means that it becomes easier and possible to will those energies to flow, without the ritual of the sexual act or any sexual contact. They can be so powerful as to stimulate sensations upon the body without any direct physical stimulation, including a sexual climax reported to be of greater intensity than physical sex.

Beyond what is feasible with the powers of the body and its energy, it would be dismissive not to assign as much meaning to like powers of the mind and the non-material aspects of life. All of the mysteries we experience throughout our lives clearly suggest that the understanding of mystical power and energies are truly at infancy at this stage of human evolution. For the scientifically minded, before you dismiss these ideas too quickly, I would recommend "The Dancing Wu Li Masters; An Overview of the New Physics, by Gary Zukav," which presents compelling parallels between mysticism and Quantum Physics.

There is much more to be understood in this realm, and hopefully more serious research can be done. I don't have sufficiently meaningful materials to release on this subject at this time. The little I share with you here is on the presumption that if you have come this far into the book, and have actually put in practice some of the drills and exercises I prescribed, it is likely you will have encountered new realms, beyond those you had already known, and the information maybe of use in your personal trek. These exercises, rituals, you might say, are workable in many other zones of life, than I at first suggest. I put them here for you with the sense that if I could help you create love, then, since Love is indeed at the core of all things creation, you would expand and emanate that aura through out all aspects of life.

    For now, let's just seed the ground with hope; and in time, we will return to the vineyard at harvest time, to reap the products of our work.

True love begins when nothing
is looked for in return.
~ Antoine De Saint-Exupery ~

Prologue
All Good Things...

Have you heard the phrase "All good things come to an end?" Let's rephrase it, "All things continue to evolve." Life is continuous transformation and as you live day by day and interact with your connections, often-unpredictable changes enter into your life and into theirs. Life is an ever-changing stream of events and conditions. As you allow yourself to experience what comes your way, whether they be events outside of your sphere of control, or those you cause to come into existence through your own power, you gain life and experience, and all that you need to progress along paths of your choice. And, yes, all good things come to those who ask for them, and those who wait, and those who act.

We have discussed many things, which sometimes appear marginal to the matter of developing and maintaining connections. To explain the relationship to what may appear marginal, I like to use the example of the Chinese doctor who was examining the patient's knee. The patient exclaimed, "Why are you looking at me knee? I came to have my elbow healed. What's the connection between my elbow and my knee?" Without shifting his procedure in the slightest and without the slightest mental flinch, the doctor replied, "Take a look."

Yes, take a look at the whole; the body, the mind, the spirit, skills, knowledge and understanding of things nearby, and those throughout the universe, all make up a whole no

part of which can be ignored without surprising consequences.
We also might have discussed many more things related to connections and relationships. I could have gone into intricate case studies and documentation and other standard academic processes that would have been ideal for an academic thesis or for a professional counselor. However, I need to make neither excuse nor apology to give you what I have and what I know is powerful wisdom.

      These words will vanish, and some of the ideas you can see to be true, will become your own, and will shape your attitude. It is my intention that you develop along paths you choose, based on your personal objectives and desires, taking into consideration how those things affect those around you as well.

You will evolve with the use of the information in this book and other sources, including your own wisdom, to the extent to which you choose to use that knowledge to help you along your road.
Begin!!

Prologue

Colophon

Text set in Georgia
Titles set in Edwardian Script ITC
using Adobe InDesign 5

Printed in USA

One Spirit Press
www.onespiritpress.com
onespiritpress@gmail.com

www.ingramcontent.com/pod-product-compliance
Lightning Source LLC
Chambersburg PA
CBHW020352170426
43200CB00005B/139